D1088897

HANSONS' AMERICAN ART POTTERY COLLECTION

identification and values

Bob & Jane Hanson

COLLECTOR BOOKS

A Division of Schroeder Publishing Co., Inc.

Left: 6" Weller vase, 1915 Orris line, $150.00 – 200.00.
Right: 7" Peters & Reed vase, Matte Shadow Ware, $200.00 – 250.00.

On the front cover: Brush-McCoy Jewel line vase, page 15; Roseville Vista umbrella stand, page 125; Muncie candlestick, page 81; McCoy Matte Green vase, page 4; Rookwood three-handled vase, page 121.

On the back cover: Brush-McCoy Moderne Kolorkraft vase, page 24; Weller Orris vase, page 2; Weller Parian vase, 7" high, $150.00 – 200.00.

Cover design by Beth Summers
Book design by Allan Ramsey

COLLECTOR BOOKS
P.O. Box 3009
Paducah, Kentucky 42002-3009

www.collectorbooks.com

Copyright © 2007 Bob & Jane Hanson

All rights reserved. No part of this book may be reproduced, stored in any retrieval system, or transmitted in any form, or by any means including but not limited to electronic, mechanical, photocopy, recording, or otherwise, without the written consent of the authors and publisher.

The current values in this book should be used only as a guide. They are not intended to set prices, which vary from one section of the country to another. Auction prices as well as dealer prices vary greatly and are affected by condition as well as demand. Online auction prices can be much higher or much lower, depending on how many people are bidding. Authors' values are based on perfect pieces with no chips, cracks, or hairlines. Neither the authors nor the publisher assumes responsibility for any losses that might be incurred as a result of consulting this guide.

Searching for a Publisher?

We are always looking for people knowledgeable within their fields. If you feel that there is a real need for a book on your collectible subject and have a large comprehensive collection, contact Collector Books.

Proudly printed and bound in the
United States of America

Contents

WPA Pottery

The Works Progress Administration (WPA) was a government-subsidized program for artists, including potters, instituted during the Depression. WPA artists received a subsistence wage for their work.

In Cleveland, Ohio, Edris Eckhardt was a key figure in the WPA, working from 1935 to 1941 in the areas of ceramic sculpture and architectural murals. For a WPA pottery project, she initiated an "Alice in Wonderland" series. She made the molds for the five sculptured pieces in the series and taught others all the steps needed to complete the figures.

Artist: Edris Eckhardt
WPA figurine, $1,500.00 – 1,700.00.
From *Alice in Wonderland*, the Walrus and the Carpenter.

Bob & Jane Hanson

10" Fulper vase, $750.00 – 950.00.
12" McCoy Matte Green vase, $300.00 – 500.00.
5½" Fulper vase, $400.00 – 550.00.

About the Authors

Bob was born in Seattle, Washington in 1943. He attended Seattle public schools and Seattle University before working as a sales representative for the General Electric Major Appliance Division. Bob married Margaret Brubacher in 1964 and they had four children that currently live in the Seattle area. Later Bob formed Hanson Sales & Marketing Company specializing in the consumer electronics field and selling to major retailers and distributors in Washington, Oregon, and Alaska. He worked in the field until his retirement in 1997.

Collecting started with Bob getting interested in electric novelty clocks in the 1980s while Margaret was busy collecting McCoy pottery, plastic jewelry, Enid Collins purses, and reverse paintings. When he had trouble finding different electric clocks to collect, Bob started to help Margaret with her pottery craze and moved into a more eclectic mode, buying all kinds of American art pottery, especially from the Arts & Crafts movement. Bob and Margaret were asked by the Huxfords to update the values in their book, *The Collector's Encyclopedia of McCoy Pottery*, and they did so with the assistance of their son, Harper Hanson. That began their extra careers as co-authors of the *McCoy Pottery Collector's Reference & Value Guides*. Margaret died of cancer in 2001.

Bob was introduced to Jane Ross Roper by his daughter, Heidi. They were married in June 2005. Jane has two adult children who live in the Seattle area. She is a practicing school psychologist with undergraduate and master's degrees from Harvard University.

Publications: *McCoy Pottery Collector's Reference & Value Guide, Volume I*
McCoy Pottery Collector's Reference & Value Guide, Volume II
McCoy Pottery Collector's Reference & Value Guide, Volume III

Dedication

This art pottery book is dedicated to the late Margaret Lea Hanson, for without her love of collecting art pottery we would never had been able to produce this book. Margaret was born in Fairbanks, Alaska, on November 12, 1942. She died of cancer on November 1, 2001.

Preface

This reference book is exclusively about art pottery produced in the United States. The book contains over 40 different manufacturers of pottery. The book is laid out in alphabetical order by factory and was put together using our collection and the collections of our friends that are acknowledged in the next few pages. We hope you find this information useful in your collecting.

Acknowledgments

We want to say thank you to the many friends that helped us so generously by sharing their knowledge and welcoming us into their homes to photograph and touch some pretty valuable pieces of pottery. We didn't damage a single piece! We also want to thank Steve and Leslie Cahn from Florida for sharing the Hull Pottery Association commemorative plaque with us.

Louie and Eleanore Geissel, Washington

Theron and Kulany Hanson, Washington

Harper Bob Hanson, Washington

Craig Nissen, Wisconsin

Phil and Laura Allhands, Oregon

Red and Mary Ann Huston, Missouri

Ikune Sawada, Washington

Ron Butler, Ohio

Roy Higgins, Ohio

Diane Eronemo, Washington

Mike Eronemo, Washington

Bob Demmink, Michigan

Mark Mulder, Michigan

Joann Shoemaker, Washington

Dirk and Stephanie Card, Ohio

Moe and Anita Jerome, Washington

Introduction

My passion for American art pottery began in the late 80s from my obsession of collecting as many different novelty electric clocks as possible. My late wife, Margaret, and our two youngest children, Harper and Hallie, would hop into the old Mercedes and off we'd go to as many antique stores and shows as we could fit into a weekend. Harper was into finding things for me to purchase while Hallie stayed close to her mother. The kids were quite young for this fun pastime and many store owners kept a careful eye on them. They never broke anything!

After awhile Margaret got tired of clocks. She thought they were boring, so she began collecting Nelson McCoy pottery. I was still looking for more novelty clocks, but after collecting about 200 of them, I was having trouble finding one we didn't already own, so I started helping Margaret collect McCoy pottery. I liked the early stoneware and especially the matte glazes, but Margaret's dream pieces were the larger animal planters and other pieces from the 50s and 60s. I began to look at other art pottery pieces from different companies and began to get more into the Arts & Crafts era pots — they are my favorite to this day. We were able to acquire enough McCoy pottery to be asked by Sharon Huxford if we would write a new McCoy reference book. With the help of a close friend and fellow McCoy collector, Craig Nissen, Margaret and I authored three volumes of the *McCoy Pottery Collector's Reference & Value Guide*.

We got to know and become friends with many antique dealers. One couple had lots of McCoy pottery for sale in their mall space, so Margaret figured they must be collectors. She asked the mall to give them our phone number, as there was a certain item she thought they might have and she wanted it pretty bad. Well, they called, she purchased the piece from them, and we became close friends. We had many antique hunts with Louie and Eleanore Geissel, enough so that Louie, a long-time pottery collector, became my mentor and helped me identify pieces that were not marked. Every time I would pick up a non-McCoy piece and look at the bottom, Margaret would scold me and tell me I was going to drop it. Louie convinced her that it was the only way to learn.

Harper, my younger son, has a great Burley Winter collection, most of which is shown in the Burley Winter section in this book. Hallie, my younger daughter, has a nice McCoy stoneware collection along with about 200 ceramic mermaids. Heidi, my older daughter, has a great assorted pottery collection, most of which she got from Margaret and me. Theron, my older son, has a nice McCoy collection that he's been given as Christmas and birthday gifts even though he acts as if he doesn't like it. I will continue to give him McCoy for Christmas and birthdays for as long as my collection holds out.

A few years after Margaret passed away, my daughter, Heidi Whaley, introduced me to Jane Roper. Jane's son and daughter-in law, Charles and Lorie Brighton, are close friends of Heidi and her husband Scott. Jane and I were married in June of 2005. Jane has undergraduate and master's degrees from Harvard University. She is a school psychologist and was able to figure me out in a hurry. Jane is the co-author of this book. Our art pottery collection has grown to over 1,500 pieces, and we're still collecting. This book contains many pieces that we own, but many more are from the collections of our old and new friends made along the way. Jane also has a daughter, Mary Brighton.

Jane and I traveled over 7,000 miles in the summer of 2005 to the pottery festival in Zanesville, Ohio, and then to stops all over the country to photograph many of the pieces within this book. A new friend, Robert (Bob) Demmink, offered to photograph a collection for the book belonging to a friend of his in Michigan. Bob did a wonderful job, and Jane and I sincerely appreciate his help.

Dirk and Stephanie Card, who live in Ohio where many of the art potteries were produced, also photographed part of their beautiful pottery collection that we've added to this book. We are very grateful to Phil and Laura Allhands for allowing us to view and photograph their collection and for giving us the benefit of their expertise and time. Mike and Diane Eronemo and Moe and Anita Jerome, four of my high school classmates, have also managed to assemble wonderful collections that they shared with us to use in the book.

American art pottery is like any other form of art; the beauty is in the eye of the beholder. Art pottery does not have to be expensive to be collected. We've collected what we've liked and tried to stay away from pieces that were damaged, but once in a while we purchased a piece and found out later it was damaged in some way.

We hope you enjoy this collection and use our book often for reference.

Zanesville Art Pottery
Zanesville, Ohio

The Zanesville Art Pottery Company was formed in 1900 when owners of the Zanesville Roofing Tile Company decided to shift from manufacturing roofing tile to pottery. The firm's president was David Schmidt, who had moved from Germany to Pittsburgh before going to Zanesville.

The art pottery of the company has been compared to that of Weller and J.W. McCoy. Some was dark brown with underglaze decorations. The company's famous art line was called La Moro. There was also a line of matte wares with slip decoration.

During both 1901 and 1910 the pottery was destroyed by fire and rebuilt. The Zanesville Art Pottery was sold to S. A. Weller in 1920.

Zanesville vase, 12½" x 4½", $125.00 – 150.00.

American Encaustic Tiling Company (AETCO)
Zanesville, Ohio

The American Encaustic Tiling Company (AETCO) was started in Zanesville, Ohio, in 1875 as a commercial tile company manufacturing tile for flooring and walls. The company's offices and owners were in New York City. AETCO was the pioneer American company in commercial tile production. The company initially both manufactured and laid its tile. The firm prospered and contemplated a move to New Jersey in 1889, but incentives from the city of Zanesville enticed the owners to change their plans and to keep production there. They opened a new plant in 1892 which was the largest tile works in the world. The firm eventually had a shop in New York City and a plant in California, in addition to the Zanesville operation.

AETCO produced a variety of art tiles while continuing to produce tile for commercial applications, such as half of the tiles used in the Holland Tunnel in New York City. The company was known for its advertising and souvenir tiles produced for businesses and political campaigns. They made artistic mantel facings and tile panels.

Frederick Hurten Rhead worked at AETCO from 1917 to 1927, first as a designer and then as head of the research department. During this time, and later, clay products other than tile were made, such as figurines and vases. Other prominent figures in American pottery who worked at AETCO include Lawton Gonder, Karl Langenbeck, and Herman Mueller.

The company fell on hard times after the stock market crash of 1929. They cut production and sold the California operation in 1932, and the Zanesville plant closed for good in 1935.

5½" lady's cuspidor, very early, $800.00 – 1,000.00.

Avon Faience Company
Wheeling, West Virginia

The Avon Faience Company was in existence under that name only during 1902 and 1903. Its previous history included changes in locale, from Ohio to Virginia; changes in ownership; and changes in name. Avon Faience art pottery was artist-decorated on solid color backgrounds. Avon Faience Company's main claim to fame is that Frederick H. Rhead, the famous art potter, worked there in 1902 and 1903. Rhead had just emigrated from England and introduced new designs and methods at Avon, such as the squeeze bag technique. In 1903, Avon became one department of the Wheeling Potteries Company. Avon made art pottery only until 1905, and the entire Wheeling Potteries firm ended in 1908.

8" tall jardiniere, 40" in circumference. Inscribed: "The glorious summer's symphony of love — laughter and life." Signed "Avon F.H." (Frederick Hurten Rhead), dated 1903, $4,800.00 – 5,200.00.

Photograph of the bottom showing the signature.

Bauer
Los Angeles, California

The J. A. Bauer Pottery was started in 1909 in Los Angeles, California, and continued until 1962. The founder, John "Andy" Bauer, was the son of John Bauer, founder of the Paducah Pottery of Paducah, Kentucky. The California company produced flowerpots, stoneware, and other practical items and made artware from around 1914 through the early 1920s. Prominent Bauer designers during this era were Louis Ipsen, a Danish designer, and Matt Carlton, a potter from Arkansas. Matte Green glazes were dominant during the period.

Bauer made a line of artware in Art Deco shapes with matte or dark glazes. Matte Green glazes on the redware body were predominant. The company won a bronze medal for its art pottery at the Panama-California Exposition in 1915 – 1916.

John "Andy" Bauer died in 1922, and by then the business had come under the control of a partnership that included his son-in-law, Watson E. Bockmon. Bockman led the company into the production of very successful casual tableware, including the "ring" and "plain" designs. The company lasted until around 1962, when it was closed by the widow of Watson E. Bockmon.

From the left: 8" x 3" Matte Green flower bowl, $250.00 – 300.00.
1¾" x 3" matching flower frog, $75.00 – 100.00.
8½" double-handled vase, $600.00 – 800.00.

15" Red-Orange glazed oil jar, $1,500.00 – 1,800.00.

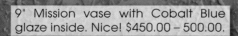

9" Mission vase with Cobalt Blue glaze inside. Nice! $450.00 – 500.00.

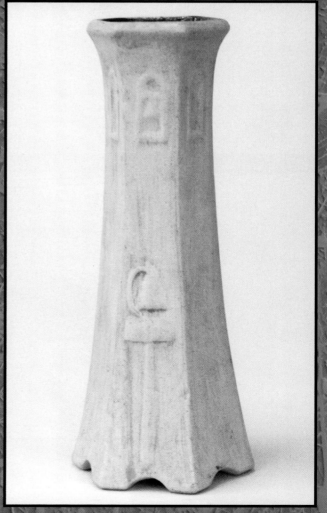

Brush-McCoy Pottery Company & J. W. McCoy Pottery Company

Roseville and Zanesville, Ohio

The history of McCoy pottery companies is complex, as it involves four generations and several different companies. The separate section in this book on the Nelson McCoy pottery company contains additional information.

J. W. McCoy was the son of W. Nelson McCoy, who had manufactured rough and unfinished pottery in the mid-nineteenth century in Putnam, Ohio, near Zanesville. He moved to Roseville, Ohio, around 1871 and opened a general store in 1876. At that time, there were many established potteries in the region, but the high demand for pottery induced him to form a new pottery company in Roseville. In 1886, J. W. McCoy added his name to the 13 established Roseville potteries with the formation of the Williams and (J. W.) McCoy Co. About 1890, they merged with another pottery and were renamed the Kildow, Williams and McCoy Pottery Co. J. W. also became a pottery jobber that supplied pottery to wholesalers and undoubtedly also retailed pottery through his general store. About two years later, the Kildow, Williams and McCoy Pottery Co. was renamed the Midland Pottery Co. In 1898, the company was sold to the Roseville Pottery Co. The next year, J. W. McCoy formed a pottery company solely under his own name. He began his pottery business by producing the same type items as before, those related to foodstuff preparation and storage. However, as early as 1904 the J. W. McCoy Pottery Company branched out into the new field of art pottery. This consisted of decorative vases, jardinieres and pedestals, umbrella stands, and flowerpots. These pieces proved to be desirable to consumers, and the new undertaking was successful. One of the earliest art pottery lines of the company was the Loy-Nel-Art line which was named after J. W. McCoy's three sons, Lloyd, Nelson, and Arthur.

George S. Brush became manager of the J. W. McCoy Pottery Co. in 1909. Brush purchased the old Owens Pottery building and its molds and equipment and sold them to McCoy in 1911, thereby acquiring a controlling interest in the J. W. McCoy Pottery Co. Soon thereafter, the business became the Brush-McCoy Pottery Company. The Brush-McCoy firm kept and used some of the Owens molds.

In 1918, the McCoy family sold its interest in the Brush-McCoy Pottery Company. However, it was not until 1925 that the McCoy name was dropped and became the Brush Pottery. It should be noted that the company continued many of the lines created before 1918 into the ensuing years. The Brush Pottery Company remained in business, with changes in ownership, until 1982.

It is often difficult to distinguish between pottery made by the J. W. McCoy Pottery and that made by Brush-McCoy. Compounding the difficulty is the fact that most pieces made by Brush-McCoy lacked identifiable marks. Sometimes the pieces were marked with a mold number.

Brush Pottery building located in Roseville, Ohio. This photo was taken in 2004.

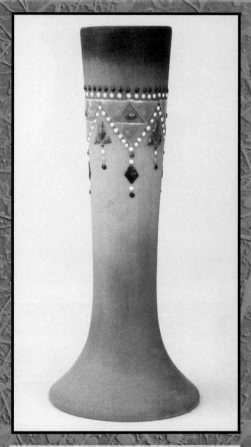

3" Jewel line vase, $400.00 – 500.00.
12" Jewel line vase, $2,500.00 – 3,000.00.

12" Jewel line vase, $800.00 – 1,200.00.

4¼" Zuniart vase, $600.00 – 700.00.
4¼" Zuniart vase, $500.00 – 600.00.
4¼" Florastone vase, $800.00 – 900.00.

Brush-McCoy Egyptian vase, scarab
design, $2,000.00 – 2,200.00.

7" J. W. McCoy Rosewood vase, $350.00 – 500.00.
11" J. W. McCoy Olympia vase, $800.00 – 900.00.
4¼" Rosewood creamer/vase, $200.00 – 250.00.

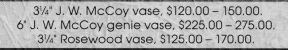

3¼" J. W. McCoy vase, $120.00 – 150.00.
6" J. W. McCoy genie vase, $225.00 – 275.00.
3¼" Rosewood vase, $125.00 – 170.00.

J. W. McCoy Loy-Nel-Art vase, $500.00 – 600.00.
Loy-Nel-Art umbrella stand, $800.00 – 1,000.00.

8" x 9" Loy-Nel-Art jardiniere, $450.00 – 550.00.

Brush-McCoy Matte Green.
8" x 9" jardiniere, $200.00 – 300.00.
2½" x 4" flower bowl, $150.00 – 200.00.
4¼" vase — nice form! $250.00 – 275.00.

Brush-McCoy Cleo vase,
$2,000.00 – 2,500.00.

Brush-McCoy Colonial Matte Green.
10" vase, $350.00 – 400.00.
6½" vase, $125.00 – 150.00.
3¼" round vase, $150.00 – 200.00.
2½" x 4" bowl, $100.00 – 125.00.

23" blended umbrella stand, $500.00 – 600.00.
28½" jardiniere & pedestal, $1,500.00 – 1,800.00.

20½" Onyx umbrella stand, $500.00 – 600.00.
24" blended jardiniere & pedestal, $700.00 – 800.00.

1910 Brush-McCoy Liberty Bell umbrella stand. Signed by A. Cusick on the side. Photos show both sides.
$800.00 – 1,000.00.

5" Amaryllis jardiniere, $100.00 – 150.00.
29" Amaryllis jardiniere & pedestal, $900.00 – 1,200.00.
11" Amaryllis vase, $150.00 – 200.00.

4½" Amaryllis vase, $125.00 – 150.00.
5" Amaryllis vase, $125.00 – 150.00.
4¼" Amaryllis vase, $125.00 – 150.00.

Amaryllis candlesticks, $150.00 – 200.00.
4¼" Amaryllis vase, $125.00 – 150.00.

7½" Amaryllis Pastel Ware bowl, $130.00 – 150.00.
9" Amaryllis Pastel Ware vase, $175.00 – 225.00.
3¼" Amaryllis Pastel Ware vase, $150.00 – 200.00.

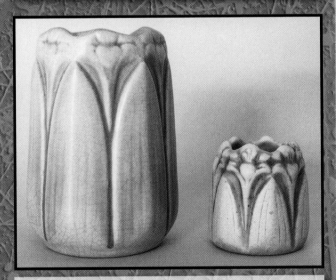

6" Pastel Ware vase, $175.00 – 225.00.
3" Pastel Ware vase, $100.00 – 125.00.

9¼" Amaryllis vase, $150.00 – 200.00.
6" Amaryllis vase, $140.00 – 175.00.
3" Amaryllis candlestick, $75.00 – 100.00.

3½" Moderne Kolorkraft vase, $75.00 – 100.00.
6" Moderne Kolorkraft vase, $150.00 – 175.00.
12" Moderne Kolorkraft vase, $250.00 – 300.00.
7" Moderne Kolorkraft vase, $160.00 – 180.00.

3½" flowerpot, $50.00 – 70.00.
2½" x 5" flower bowl, $50.00 – 75.00.
4¼" vase, $75.00 – 100.00.

8½" Glo-Art vase, $75.00 – 100.00.
6½" Glo-Art vase, $65.00 – 95.00.
4½" Glo-Art vase, $40.00 – 50.00.
3½" Glo-Art vase, $30.00 – 40.00.

12" Glo-Art vase, $100.00 – 150.00.

6½" Glo-Art vase, $65.00 – 95.00.
7" Glo-Art vase, $50.00 – 75.00.
4½" Glo-Art vase, $40.00 – 50.00.

6" Vestal Duo-Tone vase, $130.00 – 160.00.
8" Vestal Duo-Tone vase, $175.00 – 200.00.
8½" Vestal Duo-Tone vase, $200.00 – 250.00.
9" Vestal Duo-Tone vase, $225.00 – 250.00.

3" x 5½" Matte Green elephant bookends, $250.00 – 350.00.

8½" Matte Green vase, $300.00 – 400.00.

5" Colonial matte jardiniere, $40.00 – 50.00.
4½" Colonial matte candlestick, $50.00 – 60.00.

10½" musical jug, Onyx glaze, $140.00 – 165.00.
11½" Onyx urn jardiniere, $250.00 – 300.00.
8" Brown Onyx vase, $45.00 – 75.00.

12" Onyx lamp, $100.00 – 150.00.

7½" flower bowl, $30.00 – 40.00.
3½" Onyx ashtray, $20.00 – 30.00.
6" vase, $30.00 – 40.00.

Musical jug in Blue Onyx with hole, $150.00 – 200.00.
Small jug, $125.00 – 150.00.

9½" Onyx flower bowl, $60.00 – 75.00.
9" Onyx Deco-shaped vase, $200.00 – 250.00.
10½" vase (nice shape!), $100.00 – 150.00.

Matte Rust Green display.
5" vase with ears, $65.00 – 75.00.
6" flower bowl, $45.00 – 55.00.
9½" Deco vase, $175.00 – 225.00.
12" Deco vase, $250.00 – 350.00.

Art Vellum vases.
11" vase, $150.00 – 200.00.
8" vase, $75.00 – 100.00.
6" vase, $75.00 – 100.00.

8½" vase, $60.00 – 70.00.
5" Swans vase, $50.00 – 60.00.
5" jardiniere, $65.00 – 75.00.

Art Vellum flower bowl with flower frogs.
Flower bowl with frog, $100.00 – 125.00.
Vellum flower frog, $75.00 – 100.00.

5" jardiniere, $40.00 – 50.00.
8½" vase, $75.00 – 95.00.
Pair of 6" vases, $50.00 – 60.00.

9" Panel Art jardiniere, $150.00 – 200.00.
8" blended jardiniere, $75.00 – 120.00.
9½" Grapes blended jardiniere, $150.00 – 200.00.

19" Bungalow jar, $200.00 – 250.00.
18" blended umbrella stand, $250.00 – 300.00.

Brown glazed lamp, $75.00 – 100.00.

8" Bon-Ton Grapes jardiniere, $100.00 – 150.00.

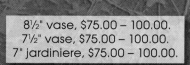

8½" vase, $75.00 – 100.00.
7½" vase, $75.00 – 100.00.
7" jardiniere, $75.00 – 100.00.

7" across double
frogs ashtray, $125.00 – 150.00.

18" frog sprinkler, $1,000.00 – 1,200.00.
2" small frog, $150.00 – 200.00.

Three hand-painted frog figurines.
10" frog, $150.00 – 250.00.
5" frog, $65.00 – 85.00.
7" frog, $100.00 – 120.00.

Two painted turtle figurines.
5" turtle, $50.00 – 75.00.
7" turtle, $100.00 – 150.00.

7" reclining frog, $150.00 – 200.00.
4" frog, $50.00 – 65.00.
7" sitting frog, $150.00 – 200.00.

Burley Winter
Crooksville, Ohio

The Burley and Winter Pottery Company, also commonly referred to as Burley Winter, was in business in Crooksville, Ohio, from 1872 to its liquidation in 1937. The company's history is complex, because there were a number of potters named Burley and a number of companies with Burley in their names. There were potters named Burley from as early as 1825 in the Crooksville, Ohio, area. William Newton Burley and Wilson Winter started Burley and Winter in 1872. The company became Burley Winter and Brown in 1885, but Brown left in 1892 and the plant became the Burley and Winter Pottery. Burley and Winter Pottery then merged with two other pottery companies (one of which was the J. G. Burley Pottery Company) around 1912 and continued until 1937. There was also the Burley Pottery Company, formed after Z. W. Burley bought the Globe Stoneware Company after 1912. The Burley Pottery Company operated until 1922, when it was sold. Z. W. Burley then teamed with his brother, Dr. S. V. Burley, to form the Burley Clay Products Company in 1923. As late as 1988 the company was still in operation under the management of grandsons of W. N. Burley. Now the Swingle family has established New Burley Winter, Inc., and is reproducing pottery items using old Burley Winter molds. The new products are marked "New Burley Winter."

Burley Winter produced a number of products over the years, including utilitarian "Heart Brand" stoneware. American art pottery lovers are attracted to Burley Winter artware, with its signature blended glaze matte finish and simple, elegant, and very artistic shapes. The pottery was rarely hand-decorated; its beauty is in its shapes and glazes. Subtle variations of the blended glazes characterize each piece of Burley Winter artware.

20" lamp, $250.00 – 300.00.
7³/₄" vase with ears, $75.00 – 100.00.
Not original shade.

28" lamp, not original shade, $300.00 – 350.00.

Lovely 16" pedestal, 10" jardiniere, jardiniere with flat flare pedestal, $1,500.00 – 2,000.00.

Rare 16" pedestal, 8" jardiniere with checkerboard top with round base pedestal, $1,500.00 – 2,000.00.

19" handled porch jar, with "V" design top, $500.00 – 600.00.

17" Dancing Ladies design, umbrella stand, $600.00 – 800.00.

18" hand-turned floor vase, with handles, $500.00 – 600.00.

19½" hand-turned floor vase, $900.00 – 1,200.00.

16" hand-turned floor vase, $500.00 – 600.00.

17" handled porch jar, $800.00 – 900.00.

12" shoulder vase (also made as a lamp), $225.00 – 250.00.
12½" handled urn vase, $200.00 – 225.00.
11¾" footed bulb vase, $225.00 – 250.00.

12" flare rim vase, $150.00 – 200.00.
11" bouquet vase, $125.00 – 150.00.
12½" trumpet-shaped vase, $150.00 – 200.00.

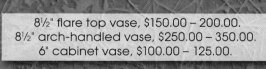

8½" flare top vase, $150.00 – 200.00.
8½" arch-handled vase, $250.00 – 350.00.
6" cabinet vase, $100.00 – 125.00.

10½" raised paisley design vase, $350.00 – 400.00.
9" Water Lily fan vase, $250.00 – 300.00.
8" applied handle vase, $300.00 – 350.00.

11" handled vase, $200.00 – 250.00.
12" bulbous vase, $250.00 – 300.00.
13" flare top vase, $350.00 – 400.00.

8½" wide shoulder vase, $200.00 – 250.00.
6½" pillow vase, $250.00 – 275.00.
8½" wide shoulder vase, $200.00 – 225.00.

Two more glazes of the wide shoulder vase.
Each, $200.00 – 225.00.

4¼" jardiniere, $100.00 – 125.00.
6¼" jardiniere, $150.00 – 175.00.
9¼" jardiniere, $250.00 – 350.00.

6¾" vase, $140.00 – 160.00.
7¾" vase, $150.00 – 175.00.
6½" vase, $120.00 – 140.00.
7¾" vase, $160.00 – 180.00.
6" vase, $120.00 – 130.00.

12" centerpiece bowl, $250.00 – 300.00.
4½" x 5½" frog, $130.00 – 150.00.

8" handled vase, $130.00 – 165.00.
4½" x 5½" frog, $130.00 – 150.00.
10" handled vase, $175.00 – 225.00.

6" handled vase, $120.00 – 150.00.
8" handled vase, $160.00 – 175.00.
4½" cabinet vase, $75.00 – 100.00.
7" handled vase, $150.00 – 165.00.

9½" vase, $150.00 – 175.00.
8½" vase, $200.00 – 225.00.
9" vase, $160.00 – 180.00.

8½" vase, $200.00 – 225.00.
12" vase, $200.00 – 250.00.

Three 7" vases, $75.00 – 100.00 each.

6½" vase, $65.00 – 85.00.
9" vase, $75.00 – 100.00.

10" vase, $200.00 – 250.00.
13" vase, $175.00 – 200.00.

4" flowerpot, $65.00 – 75.00.
3" x 7" bowl, $75.00 – 100.00.
5½" vase, $100.00 – 125.00.

6½" vase, $75.00 – 100.00.
5" vase, $100.00 – 120.00.
3½" bowl, oval, 5" x 2½", $125.00 – 150.00.

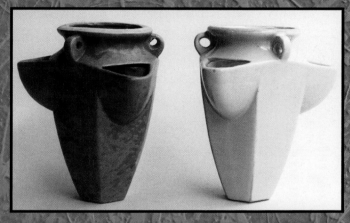

6" hanging baskets, $175.00 – 225.00 each.

6½" handled vase, $100.00 – 110.00.
8" handled vase, $120.00 – 150.00.
7½" handled vase, $100.00 – 125.00.

Two 6½" vases, left & right, $100.00 – 120.00 each.
6¼" vase, center, $110.00 – 130.00.

8" jack-o-lantern with lid,
heart-shaped mark, $450.00 – 550.00.

California Faience
Berkeley, California

California Faience was the third name of a company which started as Thomas & Bragdon in 1916. Chauncey Thomas was an artist from New York, and William Bragdon was a ceramics engineer. Although it became California Faience in 1924, pieces had been marked California Faience even before then.

The company made cast pottery and hand-pressed tiles. Art pottery examples were typically simple shapes decorated with single-color matte glazes, but the tiles were decorated with many colors, usually in matte glazes. The company made giftware in the 1920s and tiles for William Randolph Hearst's famous home, San Simeon, in 1927. Production declined during and after the Depression. Bragdon bought out Thomas in the late 1930s and eventually sold the business in the 1950s.

Tile trivet, $800.00 – 900.00.

Camark Pottery
Camden, Arkansas

The Camden Art Tile and Pottery Company was founded by Samuel J. (Jack) Carnes in Camden, Arkansas, in 1926. Its pottery is known as Camark pottery – "Cam" from Camden, "ark" from Arkansas. The first art director of Camark Pottery was John Lessell, who himself established the Art China Company of Zanesville in 1924 and later moved that company to Newark, Ohio.

Working in Ohio, John Lessell used clay from Arkansas to develop lines of art pottery for Camark. Lessell had worked at other pottery companies, such as J. B. Owens Pottery Company and Weller pottery, and he created some lines for Camark similar to lines he had made for other companies. For example, the LeCamark line resembles Weller's LaSa line. After John Lessell died in 1926, his wife and daughter headed Camark's art department. Later on, Camark hired a Muncie pottery employee to mix glazes and some Muncie lines were copied.

Camark produced art pottery until the late 1920s but the firm did not close until the 1960s.

6" Blue and Green vase, $65.00 - 85.00.
4½" Matte blended glazed vase, $45.00 – 60.00.

3¾" x 9" planter box, $45.00 – 60.00.
6" pitcher, $75.00 – 95.00.

3½" bulbous vase, $50.00 – 75.00.
6" wedding vase, $100.00 – 125.00.

2½" candleholder, $40.00 – 50.00.
6" pitcher vase, $75.00 – 100.00.

3½" matte blended vase, $35.00 – 45.00.
6¼" vase with same glaze, $75.00 – 85.00.

Catalina
Catalina Island, California

Catalina Clay Products, a project of the Santa Catalina Island Company, was in existence only ten years and was the brainchild of chewing gum magnate William Wrigley, Jr., owner of the island. During the company's first three years, it concentrated on manufacturing roofing tile and indoor tile for the Catalina Casino. After that, the company diversified its production to include a number of pottery items. Wrigley insisted that the pottery be made of local clay, even though the clay was brittle and fragile. All Catalina pottery prior to 1932 had the brown-clay body.

The pottery was known for its many and beautiful glazes, many with a satin-matte finish. Tile tables featured fauna of the island. Around 1930, dinnerware was introduced and became very popular.

After Wrigley died in 1932, other clay was imported from the mainland, but the added cost was one reason why the Catalina line was ultimately sold to the Gladding-McBean company in 1937. Gladding-McBean used the Catalina trademark until 1947.

13½" vase, $400.00 – 500.00.
Tile table, hexagonal, measures
21" across the top, $1,000.00 – 1,200.00.

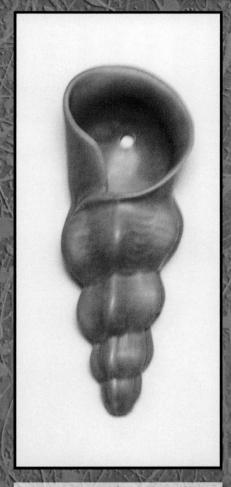

11" wall pocket, $300.00 – 450.00.

Three vases shown in various glaze colors.
5" tall and 5¾" across the handles,
$650.00 – 750.00 each.

8" handled vase, $350.00 – 450.00.
8½" wine server, $375.00 – 450.00.
3½" jardiniere, $200.00 – 225.00.
The wine server originally came with
a penguin or owl stopper.

6½" vase, $500.00 – 600.00.
The most desirable
Seafoam glaze, this vase has brown
clay. The larger sizes were not made
using the brown clay.
Marked "Catalina Island."

Cowan

Lakewood, Ohio
Rocky River, Ohio

R. Guy Cowan started his studio in Lakewood, Ohio, near Cleveland, in 1912, and the Cleveland Pottery and Tile Company, Inc., was organized in 1913 with R. Guy Cowan as president. For four years he and his artists created tile and art pottery with beautiful glazes to cover the red clay they used. The company received first prize at an International show at The Art Institute of Chicago in 1917. That same year, Cowan left to join the army and in 1919 went back to his original studio in Lakewood. The pottery was moved to Rocky River, Ohio, in 1921. At Rocky River Cowan changed from the red clay body to high-fired porcelain.

Some of Cowan's well-known artists included Waylande Gregory, Thelma Frazier, and Viktor Schreckengost. Cowan art pottery was shown at the nation's premier museums, including the Clevelend Museum of Art and the Metropolitan Museum of Art.

In 1927, the company name was changed to the Cowan Pottery Studio. The company became known for its sculpted figures but also manufactured the inexpensive Lakeware line for florists. Many of the Cowan pieces were produced in limited editions, with the molds being destroyed after the designated number of pieces were cast. The molds for the complex sculptures were intricate and made of multiple sections.

Like so many other companies after the stock market crash, Cowan had to reorganize and the company name was changed to Cowan Potters, Inc., in 1929. The company went bankrupt in 1930 and closed in 1931.

9¼" beaver candlestick #143 of 156 made for Rowfant Club, 1925, $1,000.00 – 1,200.00. 3¼" x 9¼" x 9¼" stand-up bowl, 1925, $125.00 – 150.00.

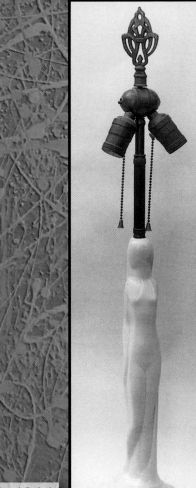

17" lamp with original finial and paper label on bottom, $850.00 – 950.00.

Dave the Slave
Edgefield, South Carolina

Although Dave the Slave does not fit exactly into the category of American art pottery, it was decided to include him as a tribute to his achievement. Dave was born around 1800 and lived in Edgefield, South Carolina. He was unusual as a slave for being able to read and write. Dave lived at one time in the household of Abner Landrum, who owned a newspaper, *The Edgefield Hive*, and taught Dave to read and write so that he could set type. It was illegal to teach slaves to read and write in most southern states.

Dave later lived in the households of John Landrum and of Lewis Miles, who was related to the Landrums.

Dave created large pieces of pottery for many years. Many of Dave's glazes have an iridescent, artistic quality. The initials "LM" are on some "Dave" pieces and stand for Lewis Miles, who is believed to have owned the pottery where Dave worked later in life.

Dave dated and sometimes signed his pieces. He even wrote short poems on certain pieces. Dave's crocks command prices in the high five-figure range.

The Philadelphia Museum of Art used a Dave the Slave crock on a poster about African-American artists that could be purchased from the museum.

Crock signed "26th April 1836," 11" tall and 10" from handle to handle.
Made before 1840. He did not sign with his name, $50,000.00 – 65,000.00.
Wouldn't you like to find one of these at a garage sale?

Fulper Pottery/Stangl Pottery
Flemington, New Jersey

The Fulper Pottery Company was incorporated in New Jersey in 1899. At the time, Fulper was primarily manufacturing utilitarian stoneware products such as casseroles, water coolers, and water filters.

William H. Fulper II, who had become plant manager in 1902, was eager to develop Fulper art pottery complementary to the Arts and Crafts styles then popular. The company's first art pottery line, Vasekraft, was introduced in 1909. Fulper produced numerous and beautiful glazes, the most expensive of which was the Famille Rose glaze. Fulper glazes were divided into a number of classes, such as Matte, Mirrored, Flambé, Lustre, and Crystal. For an extra fee, customers could specify a particular glaze rather than the glaze normally used on a particular shape. Fulper used classical forms for its art pottery inspired by Germanic, Classical, and Oriental traditions. The pottery was seldom painted or embellished.

J. Martin Stangl, a German with a master's degree in ceramic engineering, was hired by William Fulper in 1910 to superintend the technical department of the pottery. Stangl was instrumental in adding new shapes and glazes and increasing the pottery's renown. Martin Stangl and William Fulper developed the famous Fulper Vasekraft lamps, with pottery shades, in 1910 and received a patent on them in 1912.

Fulper had a contract with the Prang company to produce pottery for use as still life models for art students. These were always marked "PRANG" and still may be found.

Martin Stangl left Fulper in 1914 to work for Haeger potteries but returned to Fulper in 1920. Stangl acquired the Fulper pottery in 1930 and continued producing art pottery until 1935, after which the company's emphasis shifted to dinnerware and other items. The company's name was not officially changed to the Stangl Art Pottery Company until 1955. Stangl died in 1972 and the company was sold.

Fulper pottery was always marked but the marks are not necessarily helpful in dating the pottery. The mark is usually Fulper, Prang, or Rafco. There is often an ink-stamped vertical "Fulper" mark in a rectangle. Stangl pottery has a variety of marks. The name Stangl was even used on Fulper pottery prior to the company's name change to Stangl.

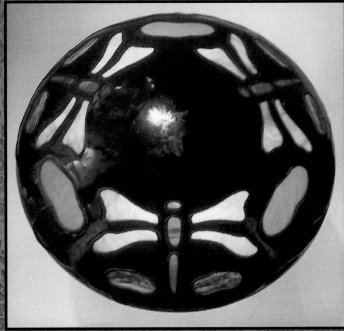

1909 – 1916 Fulper lamp with original pottery shade. Base is 17" tall, shade is 17" in diameter and 5" high.
Thirty pieces of glass make up the Dragonfly Black Gloss pottery shade, $25,000.00 – 30,000.00.
Nice to add to your collection!

Lamp, 16" tall to the top of the shade,
10" from handle to handle,
$350.00 – 450.00.

Lamp, 22" tall to the top of the
shade, $400.00 – 500.00,
3" candleholders, $100.00 – 150.00.

6" vase, $450.00 – 500.00.
8½" vase, $500.00 – 600.00.
7½" vase, $425.00 – 550.00.

4" candlestick, $140.00 – 180.00.
7" flower bowl, $200.00 – 250.00.
5" flower frog frog, $150.00 – 250.00.

11" vase, $1,500.00 – 2,000.00
9½" vase, $2,000.00 – 2,500.00

8½" bulbous vase, $450.00 – 550.00.
6½" bulbous vase, $500.00 – 600.00.
7½" bulbous vase, $450.00 – 550.00.

12½" tapered vase, $1,000.00 – 1,200.00.
15" handled vase, $900.00 – 1,000.00.
11½" handled vase, $800.00 – 900.00.

7" flower bowl, $800.00 – 900.00.
3" flower frog frog, $100.00 – 125.00.

4¼" vase, $150.00 – 200.00.
4" vase, $125.00 – 150.00.
Lily pad candleholder, $175.00 – 200.00.
4" ribbed vase, $150.00 – 165.00.

10" vase, $250.00 – 350.00.

Two 10" vases,
$700.00 – 800.00 each.

11" wall pocket, $1,000.00 – 1,200.00.

3" candleholder, $125.00 – 150.00.
4" handled vase, $145.00 – 165.00.
8½" musical jug, $200.00 – 250.00.

7" vase, $250.00 – 350.00 (nice form).
Two 6" vases, original paper labels,
$300.00 – 400.00 each.

9" handled vase, $450.00 – 500.00.

3" toothpick holder, $100.00 – 125.00.
3½" handled vase, $200.00 – 250.00.

8" handled vase, $300.00 – 400.00.
4" tapered vase, $150.00 – 200.00.

4" pillow vase, $175.00 – 200.00.

2¼" candlestick, $250.00 – 300.00.

4½" Prang vase, $300.00 – 400.00.

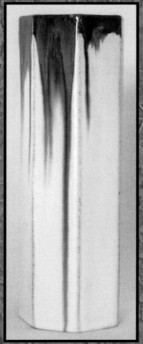

9" six-sided vase, $275.00 – 350.00.

4½" candleholder, $70.00 – 100.00.

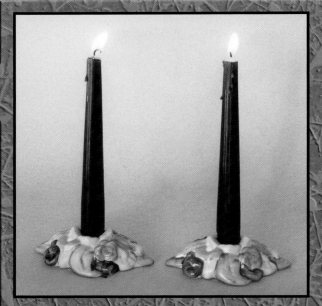

Pair of candleholders, 5" across, $150.00 – 200.00.

4" lily pad flower frog, $125.00 – 175.00.
5" scarab flower frog, $250.00 – 300.00.

5" handled vase, $50.00 – 75.00.

6½" Deco-styled vase, looks
early, as if some of the good Fulper glazes
were still being used, $150.00 – 275.00.

Grueby Pottery
Boston, Massachusetts

William H. Grueby founded the Grueby Faience Company in Boston in 1894, and the company was incorporated in 1897. In 1907, the Grueby Pottery Company was incorporated, with Grueby as president, while the Grueby Faience Company continued under different management. The change separated the two divisions of the company. The Grueby Faience Company went bankrupt in 1909, after which Grueby established the Grueby Faience and Tile Company. The Grueby Pottery closed in 1910 or 1911. William Grueby directed the operation of the Grueby Faience and Tile Company until 1912 or 1913, when it burned. Thereafter, the company continued to operate, with various changes in management, ownership, and location, until 1938. Grueby pottery was produced only until about 1909.

William Grueby attended the Chicago World's Fair in 1893 and saw European pottery. He was especially infiuenced by the French artist Delaherche, with whom he corresponded. After attending the fair, Grueby spent several years perfecting his own matte glazes, of which Matte Green became most popular. These glazes were a departure from the standard glazes prevalent in the early twentieth century. They were widely imitated by pottery manufacturers, whose products were less expensive than the handmade Grueby pottery.

Major designers at Grueby were George Prentiss Kendrick and Addison B. LeBoutillier. Young female art school graduates did most of the modeling and decorating of Grueby pottery.

Grueby's pottery often was decorated with botanically correct leaf and flower motifs which were modeled and incised by the potter. The pottery was handmade and elegant; it exemplified the values of the Arts and Crafts movement. No two pieces were identical. Grueby was associated with furniture manufacturer Gustav Stickley, who featured Grueby pottery in Stickley catalogs. He also collaborated with Tiffany by making lamp vases for Tiffany's glass lamp shades. Grueby also manufactured beautiful decorated tiles. Grueby pottery was recognized with awards at national and international expositions.

4" x ½" scarab flower frog, marked "Grueby Faience Co. Boston, USA," $750.00 – 1,000.00.

Haeger Potteries, Inc.

Macomb and Dundee, Illinois

David Haeger was the owner of the Dundee Brick Yard in Dundee, Illinois, and manufactured bricks and tiles. After his death, his sons began to produce pottery and founded Haeger potteries, Inc. Martin Stangl left the Fulper pottery of Flemington, New Jersey and assisted Haeger in developing its commercial artware; he left Haeger and returned to Fulper in 1919. Marshall Field and Company in Chicago was a major customer of Haeger's.

Many famous artists designed pieces for Haeger over the years. One of the most famous was Royal Hickman, who joined the company in 1938 and stayed until 1944, when he opened his own business in Florida. Hickman designed a black panther figurine which was widely copied by others. Another Haeger artist was Eric Olsen, who designed the Haeger animal figurine of a bull, in red or black.

Haeger figurine collection.
11½" girl, $45.00 – 50.00.
12" boy, $45.00 – 50.00.
8" seated girl, $50.00 – 60.00.
16¼" mother, $75.00 – 125.00.

10" Matte Green lady vase, $45.00 – 60.00.

15½" one-eyed Egyptian
cats, #758. Each, $150.00 – 175.00.

Royal Haeger Peacock glaze.
15" vase, 1915, $150.00 – 200.00.
16" vase, #493, $250.00 – 300.00.
18½" ewer, #408, $200.00 – 250.00.

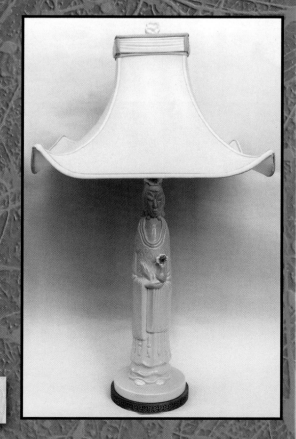

Pair of original lamps, complete with Pagoda shades (see right photo).
Male figure is 22½". With fixture, 38". Female figure is 23½" and 38" with fixture.
Designed by Mr. Eric Olsen, first produced in 1947, $575.00 – 650.00 each.

Hampshire Pottery
Keene, New Hampshire

Hampshire Pottery, begun by James Scolly Taft, began as a manufacturer of utilitarian products but by the late 1870s was making Majolica pieces. The pottery was located in Keene, New Hampshire, an area with large deposits of feldspar and clay. The company began producing more decorative pottery in 1880s. The plant was closed during part of World War I but reopened after the war and continued business until 1923.

A Royal Worcester-type ware, with a pale cream finish, was the mainstay of Hampshire's specialty ware. Hampshire pottery was decorated primarily with transfer designs, although some was hand-decorated and signed.

Hampshire's Matte Green finish was also popular.

The head artist at Hampshire was Wallace L. King. Another strong contributor to the pottery's success was Cadmon Robertson, a chemist who began working there in 1904 and became superintendent. He introduced a large number of matte glazes and colors for a variety of art pottery items. Both foreign and domestic clays were used by Hampshire.

The founder, James Scolly Taft, sold the pottery in 1916 to George M. Morton. Morton continued production for a year, but the pottery was closed in 1917 during WWI. It reopened after the war, with an emphasis on utilitarian rather than art pottery, but had to close permanently in 1923.

6" vase, $500.00 – 700.00.
6½" vase, $400.00 – 500.00.
5½" bowl, $350.00 – 400.00.
8" vase, $550.00 – 650.00.
6" serpent-handled vase,
$450.00 – 550.00.

7" patterned vase, $1,200.00 – 1,400.00.
3½" candlestick, $250.00 – 300.00.
7½" vase, $1,500.00 – 1,800.00.
7" handled chamberstick, $200.00 – 250.00.

Hull Pottery
Crooksville, Ohio

The A. E. Hull Pottery Company was founded by Addis Emmet Hull in 1905. Two years later, the company expanded by purchasing the Acme pottery. The company sold pottery all over the country and imported European pottery as well, during the 1920s. Over the years the company manufactured utilitarian wares and stoneware but in 1917 the company began making art pottery and continued to do so until the early 1950s. Addis E. Hull, Jr., became president of the company after his father's death in 1930 and kept it going through the Depression years, when many other potteries failed. He left the company in 1937 and was succeeded by Gerald F. Watts. By 1925 the company was making more than three million pieces of pottery a year, and the company continued in operation until it was destroyed by fire in 1950. It was rebuilt by 1952 and renamed Hull Pottery Company. The company finally closed in 1985.

Hull manufactured many products over the years, from stoneware to kitchenware to artware. Hull art pottery flourished during the late 1930s and 1940s. Lines often had a flower name, such as Iris, Dogwood, or Poppy. The same shapes often appeared in various lines, and the same item in a given line was often manufactured in several sizes. The Red Riding Hood character was very popular, and the Red Riding Hood cookie jar was patented.

Hull is best known for its pastel tinted artware with flower decoration and matte glazes, most of which was manufactured during the 1940s. After the company's destruction by fire in 1950, it was unable to reproduce all of the popular matte glazes that had been so popular. Two artware lines produced during the 1950s were Continental and Tropicana. Tropicana, made in seven shapes, is highly collectible.

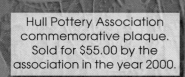

Hull Pottery Association commemorative plaque. Sold for $55.00 by the association in the year 2000.

Photograph of the welcome sign on the highway leading into Crooksville.

20" umbrella stand, made by Acme, proceeded Hull. Made by co-workers for retiring foreman Mr. Hicks. One-of-a-kind with an unknown value.

5½" x 4½" sign, $95.00 – 120.00.

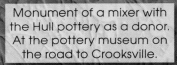

Monument of a mixer with the Hull pottery as a donor. At the pottery museum on the road to Crooksville.

Early Hull pottery,
9" vase, $115.00 – 140.00.
8" vase, $100.00 – 125.00.
6½" jardiniere, $150.00 – 175.00.

Plaque at base of the monument above.

Rare Tropicana line showing all seven of the pieces produced.

10" ashtray, $350.00 – 450.00.
8½" flat vase, $350.00 – 475.00.
12½" ewer, $575.00 – 680.00.

12½" pitcher vase, $450.00 – 550.00.
12¾" fancy basket, $750.00 – 850.00.

14½" planter vase, $675.00 – 800.00.
15½" flower bowl, $350.00 – 450.00.

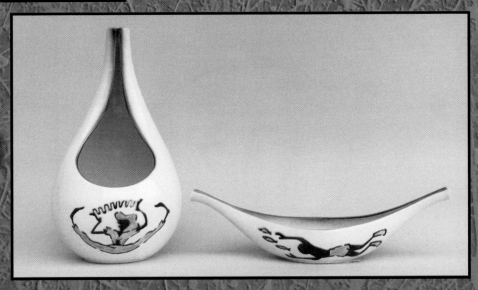

Open Rose collection.
6¼" vase, #127, $125.00 – 150.00.
12" vase, #124, $450.00 – 550.00.
7" pitcher, #105, $250.00 – 300.00.

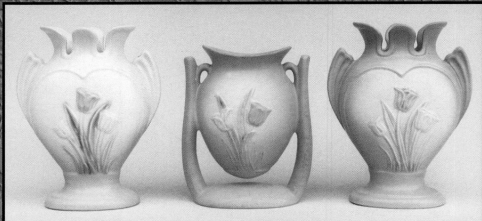

Tulip collection.
8" vase, #105-33, $250.00 – 325.00.
6" vase, #103-33, $325.00 – 375.00.
8" vase, #105-33, $250.00 – 325.00.

Pair of Dancing Lady planters.
7½" x 5" x 3½" deep.
Very Deco in design, $50.00 – 75.00 each.

Woodland collection.
8½" vase, $250.00 – 300.00.
10½" basket, $275.00 – 325.00.
6" x 11" cornucopia, $125.00 – 130.00.

Woodland collection.
3½" candleholders, $140.00 – 175.00 each.
14" console bowl, $400.00 – 500.00.

Water Lily Gloss collection.
9½" vase, $250.00 – 300.00.
8½" vase, $240.00 – 290.00.
6½" vase, $135.00 – 160.00.

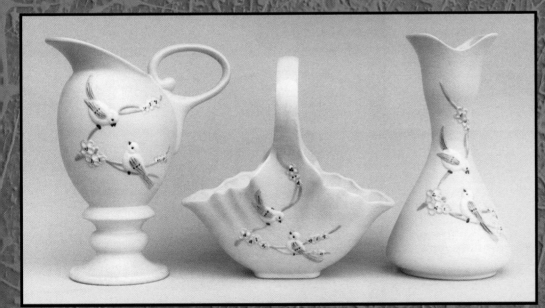

Serenade collection.
13" pitcher, $400.00 – 450.00.
12" basket, $375.00 – 425.00.
14" vase, $225.00 – 250.00.

Magnolia & Wildflower collection.
8½" cornucopia, $175.00 – 225.00.
6½" vase, $200.00 – 250.00.
8½" vase, $300.00 – 350.00.

Magnolia collection.
8½" vase, $150.00 – 200.00.
12" double cornucopia, $225.00 – 300.00.
7" pitcher, $200.00 – 250.00.

Magnolia collection.
6½" vase, $100.00 – 125.00.
15" vase, $600.00 – 650.00.
10½" vase, $225.00 – 275.00.

Continental collection.
12½" pitcher, $150.00 – 200.00.
11" cat vase, $150.00 – 200.00.
13¾" vase, $125.00 – 150.00.

Jugtown Pottery
Seagrove, North Carolina

There is a long tradition of making utilitarian pottery in the state of North Carolina, going back to the eighteenth century. Most of these potteries were, or are, in the Seagrove area in south-central North Carolina, in Piedmont.

In 1915, Juliana and Jacques Busbee began trying to revive interest in North Carolina pottery production. They started Jugtown pottery in North Carolina and sold it in their tearoom in Greenwich Village in New York City. Their best-known potter was Ben Owen, whom they hired in 1923. Jacques Busbee died in 1947, and Juliana Busbee

continued to run the pottery until 1959. After the Busbee era, Jugtown pottery continued in operation under the direction of various owners until at least 1985.

Jugtown pottery was handmade and characterized by simple but beautiful shapes. It was handmade from local clay, some red and some buff-colored. A number of glazes were made for the pottery, including one called "Tobacco Spit." Most of the pottery was undecorated. During the Busbee era Chinese-style pottery was also made.

13¼" Black candlesticks impressed with round Jugtown mark, $250.00 – 300.00 pair.
14" x 9" Black double-handled vase, $475.00 – 550.00.

Lonhuda Pottery
Steubenville, Ohio

The Lonhuda Pottery was founded by William Long and began regular production of art pottery in 1892. The name "Lonhuda" combined the names of the company's three organizers — Long, Hunter, and Day.

Lonhuda pottery was hand-decorated with hand-painted slipware underglaze. Laura Fry was probably the most famous decorator to work at Lonhuda. She had worked at Rookwood and was well-known for her patented process of applying decoration to pottery using an atomizer.

In 1894, the Weller Pottery Company acquired an interest in Lonhuda pottery. Samuel Weller and William Long formed a company known as the Lonhuda Faience Company in 1895. Fire destroyed the plant within a year, and Long left to work for the J. B. Owens Company of Zanesville. Weller rebuilt the factory and eventually renamed the Lonhuda line Louwelsa.

7" hand-painted jar jardiniere with the shield mark on the bottom. It has three legs and is decorated with thistles around the top, $400.00 – 500.00.

Marblehead Pottery
Marblehead, Massachusetts

Dr. Herbert J. Hall founded Marblehead Pottery in 1904. He also ran a sanatorium in Marblehead and thought that work at the pottery would be good therapy for the mentally ill patients. The patients were instructed in pottery and other crafts.

One of the instructors at Marblehead was Arthur E. Baggs. The pottery ended its connection with the sanitarium around 1908 and Baggs became first the director, and later the owner, in 1915. Baggs went on to work at Ohio State University and elsewhere but always came back to work summers at Marblehead until its closure in 1936.

Marblehead Pottery was always a small company. The hand-thrown pottery was usually made with muted matte glazes and simple, classical shapes. The most famous glaze was Marblehead blue, a deep gray-blue matte glaze. Some of the pottery was hand-carved. The earlier pottery was characterized by geometric designs, whereas later there were more natural and realistic decorations such as ships, birds, and flowers. Some bowls were enameled inside with a different color from the exterior.

5" x 6¾" decorated wall pocket, $3,500.00 – 4,500.00.

Nelson McCoy
Roseville, Ohio

In 1910, four years before his death, J. W. McCoy assisted his son Nelson McCoy in establishing the new Nelson McCoy Sanitary Stoneware Company in Roseville, Ohio. The new pottery specialized in utilitarian stoneware. This company was in competition with the Brush-McCoy Company, although Brush-McCoy concentrated more on decorative pieces. The early pottery of the Nelson McCoy Stoneware Company was designed mainly by Walter Bauer, including the Leaves & Berries pattern.

Around 1933, with demand for stoneware decreasing and the demand for decorative pieces on the rise, the company simplified its name to the Nelson McCoy Pottery Co. and Nelson McCoy changed the design of its products to a more artware type of pottery. In 1934, McCoy hired Sidney Cope, an Englishman, who ultimately replaced Walter Bauer as designer. Cope held this position until his death in 1961. He designed many of the popular pieces today, including the hunting dog planter; the Liberty Bell planter; and the wishing well planter. After his death, his son Leslie became the designer until 1966 when Billie McCoy took over as head of the design group.

The Nelson McCoy Pottery Co. flourished in the 1940s. Some of the floral vases were released with great success. The wishing well and spinning wheel planters were also great contributors to a very profitable time for the company.

In 1945, Nelson McCoy died and was replaced as president by his nephew, Nelson McCoy Melick. In 1950, all the manufacturing buildings were destroyed by fire, but the McCoy family decided to rebuild, utilizing the latest technology which helped position the company for the future. McCoy was the largest producer of pottery in the U.S. by the end of the decade, shipping millions of pieces annually. Mr. Melick remained as president until his death in 1954. At that time, Nelson McCoy, Jr., who had joined the company in 1948 after serving in WWII, became president, a position he held for almost three decades.

The Nelson McCoy Pottery Co. operated for 57 years until sold in 1967 to the Mount Clemens Pottery Co., which retained the Nelson McCoy pottery name and continued to run under the leadership of Nelson McCoy, Jr. For a short period after purchase, the "McCoy" name was not included on the pottery and instead some pieces were marked "MCP." The company was again sold in 1974 to Lancaster Colony Corporation (LCC). Nelson McCoy, Jr. remained as president and the pottery continued to carry the Nelson McCoy name. Nelson McCoy, Jr. left the company in 1981 after 33 years of service. In 1985, with declining sales, Lancaster was sold to Designer Accents, which merged the company with two other small companies but was not very successful and closed the doors around 1990.

7" parrot pitchers from 1952, #1573.
$175.00 – 225.00 each.
(Black plastic pin for fun).

18" floor vases from the 1930s in all the glaze colors produced.
Also known as the "Sand Dollar vase," $300.00 – 600.00 each.

1930s centerpiece bowl, $50.00 – 80.00.
Matching candleholders, $35.00 – 50.00 each.

1930s centerpiece bowl, $55.00 – 85.00.
Matching candleholders, $35.00 – 50.00 each.

1930s vase collection.
10", $90.00 – 125.00.
8", $50.00 – 90.00.
6", $40.00 – 75.00.
5", $40.00 – 75.00.

9" jardiniere & 13" pedestal, $400.00 – 500.00.

8½" jardiniere & 12½" pedestal, $250.00 – 350.00.
7" jardiniere & 6½" pedestal, $225.00 – 275.00.
10½" jardiniere & pedestal, $650.00 – 750.00.

Jardiniere collection.
7½", $100.00 – 125.00.
7", $70.00 – 95.00.
5", $55.00 – 75.00.
4", $45.00 – 70.00.

Two 7" jardinieres, $100.00 – 150.00 each.

Two 7" jardinieres, $50.00 – 75.00 each.

Two 20" McCoy sand jars
Sand Butterfly pattern,
$900.00 – 1,000.00 each.

14" x 10" sand jars, 1940s, $250.00 – 300.00.

12" floor vase with handles, $125.00 – 175.00.
12" vase without handles, $250.00 – 300.00.

12" vase, $300.00 – 500.00.

Three sizes of vases.
9", $125.00 – 175.00.
8", $80.00 – 100.00.
6", $60.00 – 80.00.

Two Basket Weave jardinieres.
7½", $75.00 – 100.00.
10½", $125.00 – 175.00.

Three swallows jardinieres.
7" jardinieres, $100.00 – 125.00 each.
4" jardiniere, $45.00 – 65.00.

Leaves & Berries lamp, $150.00 – 200.00.

Flower design lamp,
$150.00 – 200.00.

21-year-old Fergie & jars.
14" x 10" sand jar, $150.00 – 300.00.
10" x 11" porch jar, $250.00 – 300.00.

Two umbrella stands, $250.00 – 350.00 each.

18" sand jar with ears,
$1,800.00 – 2,500.00.

Two McCoy vases.
8" Burgundy, $60.00 – 75.00.
8" Brown/Green, $400.00 – 450.00.

Two hard-to-find jardinieres, $250.00 – 300.00 each.

Two 14" floor vases, $350.00 – 600.00 each.
7" jardiniere, $150.00 – 175.00.

Three Green vases.
9" vase with ears, $80.00 – 100.00.
7½" ringed vase, $100.00 – 120.00.
8" vase with ears, $100.00 – 125.00.

Three 9" Lizard handled vases,
$450.00 – 550.00 each.

Leaves & Berries pattern.
8" vase, $75.00 – 95.00.
Two 7" vases, $85.00 – 100.00 each.

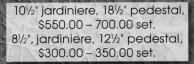

9½" jardiniere, 14½" pedestal,
$300.00 – 450.00 set.

10½" jardiniere, 18½" pedestal,
$550.00 – 700.00 set.
8½", jardiniere, 12½" pedestal,
$300.00 – 350.00 set.

10" vase, $90.00 – 110.00.
12" vase, $200.00 – 300.00.
10" vase, $110.00 – 150.00.

Jardinieres & pedestals.
8½"/12½", $300.00 – 400.00.
7½" jardiniere, $60.00 – 75.00.
10½"/18½", $450.00 – 550.00.

11" x 9½" porch jars, $225.00 – 300.00 each.

Two jardiniere & pedestal sets. 10½" jardinieres, 18" pedestals, $450.00 – 550.00 each.

Three Leaves & Berries lamps, $100.00 – 150.00 each.

20" lamp table in Green Onyx. Only two are known to exist! In 1995 one sold for over $10,000.00.

Two round lamps, $100.00 – 125.00 each.

7½" jardinieres, $45.00 – 60.00 each. 9" jardiniere, 13" pedestal, $250.00 – 300.00.

Cameo jardinieres & pedestals.
10" jardiniere, 18½" pedestal, $700.00 – 800.00.
8½" jardiniere, 12½" pedestal, $300.00 – 400.00.

Onyx Holly jardinieres & pedestals.
8½" jardiniere, 12½" pedestals, $300.00 – 350.00.
10½" jardiniere, 18½" pedestal, $550.00 – 700.00.

Two ringed jardiniere & pedestal sets.
Both have a 10½" jardiniere, and an 18½" pedestal,
$450.00 – 550.00 each.

8" jardiniere, 12½" pedestal, $300.00 – 350.00.
7" jardiniere, $75.00 – 100.00.
Green pedestal, $150.00 – 200.00.

Pictured here is the entire Butterfly line produced by McCoy.

10" handled vase, $150.00 – 225.00.
8½" fernery, $40.00 – 50.00.
5½" fernery, $30.00 – 40.00.
7½" butterfly vase, $90.00 – 110.00.
9" fernery, $75.00 – 100.00.
7" wall pocket, $250.00 – 600.00.
14" platter, $300.00 – 600.00.
6½" hanging basket, $125.00 – 300.00.
10" pitcher vase, $125.00 – 200.00.
5½" jardiniere, $100.00 – 150.00.
3¾" jardiniere, $70.00 – 90.00.

7½" jardiniere, $100.00 – 150.00.
4½" jardiniere, $40.00 – 50.00.
3½" jardiniere, $30.00 – 40.00.
9" vase, $80.00 – 125.00.
7" Castlegate vase, $125.00 – 200.00.
11" console bowl, $60.00 – 80.00.
8¼" vase, $50.00 – 80.00.
6¼" vase, $30.00 – 45.00.
8½" console bowl, $60.00 – 80.00.
4½" Ivy vase, $50.00 – 90.00.
5" console bowl, $60.00 – 80.00.
6½" flowerpot, $80.00 – 100.00.
5" flowerpot, $50.00 – 75.00.
3¾" flowerpot, $40.00 – 50.00.

Jardiniere & pedestal set.
41" tall, $1,000.00 – 1,200.00.

10½" jardiniere, 18½" pedestal, $650.00 – 750.00.
8½" jardiniere, 12½" pedestal, $250.00 – 350.00.

Two jardiniere & pedestal sets.
Both have an 8½" jardiniere and a
12½" pedestal, $200.00 – 300.00 each.

Two 15" oil jars, one 18" oil jar.
15" jars, $250.00 – 300.00 each.
18" jar, $400.00 – 450.00.

12" and 4" oil jars.
12" jar, $125.00 – 200.00.
4" jars, $40.00 – 60.00 each.

One 18" oil jar & one 15" oil jar.
18" jar, $350.00 – 450.00.
15" jar, $250.00 – 300.00.

Collection of duck pitchers, 7" tall, $90.00 – 125.00 each.

Two 10" vases, $125.00 – 175.00 each.
7" fernery, $45.00 – 60.00.

8" Cobalt Blue vase, $60.00 – 80.00.

16" sphinx sand jar, $2,000.00 – 3,000.00.

9" sailboat vase, $75.00 – 100.00.
10" vase, $125.00 – 150.00.
8" vase, $65.00 – 85.00.

8" vase, $70.00 – 90.00.
7½" vase, $100.00 – 140.00.
8" vase, $65.00 – 85.00.

Two 10" lily bud vases, $100.00 – 150.00 each.
8" lily bud vase, $65.00 – 85.00.

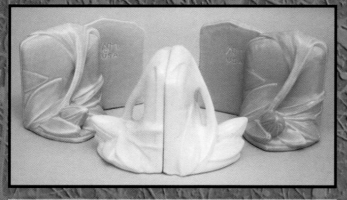

Lily bud bookends, $150.00 – 200.00 each.

6" bird bookends, $175.00 – 250.00 each set.

Early jardiniere collection.
4½", $30.00 – 50.00 each.
10", $90.00 – 110.00.

Late 1950s ribbed vases.
12", $80.00 – 100.00.
14", $110.00 – 130.00.
10", $60.00 – 70.00.

Rare 1949 fish pitchers, $900.00 – 1,100.00 each.

8" Leaves & Berries design vase, $70.00

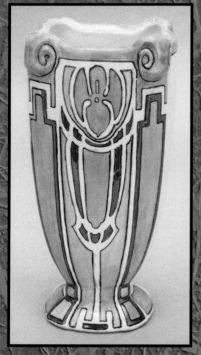

9" vase, hand-decorated under the glaze, $300.00 – 350.00.

6¾" Target vase, $100.00 – 150.00.

9" Hobnail "V" vase, $125.00 – 150.00.

Two nice vases, $100.00 – 140.00 each.

Wonderful 6½" hanging basket, $45.00 – 60.00.

McCoy Floraline fineforms.
8" vase, $40.00 – 50.00.
12" vase, $50.00 – 75.00.
8" vase, $50.00 – 60.00.

More Floraline fineforms.
11" vase, $50.00 – 75.00.
12" vase, $50.00 – 75.00.
8" vase, $50.00 – 75.00.

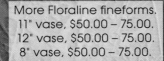

McCoy Floraline fineforms.
6" vase, $40.00 – 65.00.
12" vase, $50.00 – 75.00.
7½" vase, $50.00 – 75.00.

Floraline fineform collection.
11" x 10" x 4½" vases, $50.00 – 75.00 each.

Two 21" early umbrella stands.
(They come in handy in Seattle),
$350.00 – 400.00 each.

McCoy miniatures collection.
3" aqua cat, $350.00 – 500.00.
1½" rabbit, $300.00 – 450.00
3" pelican, $250.00 – 350.00.

Two 9½" ram's head vases, $150.00 – 200.00 each.

9" petal vase from 1955, $175.00 – 250.00.

1940s stretch animal collection.
8¼" hound, $175.00 – 225.00.
7½" dog, $200.00 – 250.00.
7½" lion, $250.00 – 350.00.
5½" ramming goat, $225.00 – 275.00.

Merrimac Pottery Company
Newburyport, Massachusetts

Thomas Nickerson started the Merrimac Ceramic Company in 1897. He had studied with chemist Sir William Crookes in England and was influenced by him. Nickerson changed the company's name in 1902 to the Merrimac Pottery Company. The change in name went hand-in-hand with a change from everyday to more artistic products.

Merrimac Pottery was characterized by simple shapes and colors, mostly hand-thrown, with no additional decoration. Glazes ranged from Matte Greens to metallic and iridescent enamels. The company made a line of Etruscan pieces modeled on pottery from ancient Roman times. The pottery was deep red with decorations in low relief.

The pottery burned down in 1908 and the remaining stock was sold. Apparently it had not been in operation for some time.

Merrimac is a Native American word for sturgeon. It is also the name of the river in Newburyport, Massachusetts.

Two examples of Merrimac vases.
11½" vase, $2,000.00 – 3,000.00.
10" vase, volcanic glaze, $3,000.00 – 5,000.00.

Metlox
Manhattan Beach, California

Theodore Prouty and his son Willis Prouty founded the Proutyline Products Company in the early 1920s. They developed and patented craze-proof "Hermosa Tile," made mostly of talc from Death Valley. Prouty sold the company to American Encaustic Tiling Company (AETCO) in 1926.

The next year, 1927, Theodore Prouty started Metlox potteries. The company did not make tiles; it started out making durable ceramic outdoor advertising signs which could be wired and lit with neon. Prouty died in 1931, and his son Willis changed the company's emphasis to dinnerware.

Before World War II, the company made some artware. Their principal artware designer was Carl Romanelli. Romanelli, working in the late 1930s and early 1940s, created the Metlox figurines of animals and novelties, and also the artware line called Modern Masterpieces. Modern Masterpieces included elegant sculptures of dancing girls, nudes, and animals, as well as functional pieces such as vases and bookends with figures in relief. Romanelli's name was typically impressed in the bases of his pieces.

During the war Metlox manufactured airplane parts, and after the war the company focused on dinnerware with great success. The company was purchased by Evan Shaw around 1947. He passed away in 1980 and his son-in-law and daughter carried on the business, finally closing the company in 1989.

Examples of Carl Romanelli modern masterpieces.
8½" Cornucopia Maid, #1805, $300.00 – 350.00.
9¾" Dancing Girl, #1806, $300.00 – 375.00.
10½" Dancing Girl, #1825, $325.00 – 400.00.

Muncie
Muncie, Indiana

The Muncie Clay Products Company began as a subsidiary of the Gill Clay Pot Company from Bellaire, Ohio, that had moved to Muncie, Indiana, in the early part of the twentieth century. Charles Grafton was president of the company. The Muncie Clay Products Company was formed in 1919 and began producing very soft glazes and beautiful forms of art pottery using matte glazes and shapes. In 1931 the company changed its name to Muncie Potteries, Inc., and lasted until 1939.

Designer Boris Trifonoff was responsible for many of the soft matte glazes produced after 1923. Some of the most desirable pieces sold by Muncie Pottery, such as those in the Ruba Rhombic line, were designed by Reuben Haley. Haley designed vases, planters, and lamps. Muncie produced pottery lamps bases for companies such as the Aladdin Lamp Company, as well as for Muncie itself. Another prominent figure at Muncie was James Wilkins, who is credited with creating many of Muncie's unusual glazes. Muncie pottery was sometimes advertised as "Rainbow" art pottery because of its varied colored glazes.

Muncie pottery is both marked and unmarked. It was around 1927 that Muncie decided to stamp the Muncie name on the bottom of its work. Before that there were sometimes capital letter marks indicating the finisher, or numbers indicating the molders. These marks were part of a piecework wage plan that enabled identification of individual workers' pieces. Very early Muncie pottery was sometimes unmarked.

17" Matte Green over Rose floor vase, $600.00 – 750.00.

9" Matte Blue over Rose candlestick, $300.00 – 350.00.

81

8" Green over Lilac vase, $125.00 – 150.00.
7" Rose vase, 1927, $200.00 – 300.00.

Green over Rose collection.
8" vase, $125.00 – 150.00.
6" vase, $75.00 – 100.00.
5½" jardiniere, $300.00 – 400.00.
5½" vase, $150.00 – 200.00.

Reuben Haley designed Ruba Rhombic Line collection.

5" Green/Lilac vase, $600.00 – 700.00.
5" Green/Lilac vase, $550.00 – 650.00.

6¼" Matte Green pillow vase, $750.00 – 850.00.

Green over Pumpkin collection.

5" Ruba Rhombic vase, $550.00 – 650.00.
5" candlestick, $150.00 – 200.00.

7" vase, $175.00 – 200.00.
4" vase, $100.00 – 125.00.

23½" table lamp, $500.00 – 600.00.

Close-up of lamp base.

18½" Lovebirds table lamp, $400.00 – 500.00.

Close-up of Lovebirds finial.

23" Aqua table lamp. Pattern of five naked male archers hunting five birds, $500.00 – 600.00.

Close-up of lamp base.

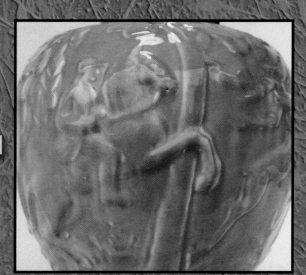

Niloak Pottery
Benton, Arkansas

J. H. Hyten was a potter who moved from Iowa to Arkansas and purchased a pottery in 1885. Hyten died soon thereafter and his eighteen-year-old son Charles took over the business. Two other sons joined the enterprise. It was called Hyten Bros. pottery.

Arthur Dovey, an artist, joined the company in 1909 and introduced Mission Ware, the line for which Niloak is most famous. The swirl ware involved the use of several different-colored clays which were formed on a potter's wheel. Every piece was different. Early pieces were completely glazed, but later the outer glaze was dropped to keep the natural look of the clays. Manufacture of the pottery was complex because of the varying chemical reactions of different clays. Charles Hyten perfected and patented the process. Hyten marketed the company's artware under the name, "Niloak," and the company then became the Niloak Pottery Company around 1911.

In the late 20s or early 30s Niloak introduced the Hywood line, which was less expensive than Mission Ware and was, for the most part, cast in molds. The pottery was marked with the Hywood name at first but eventually marked as Niloak.

Sales declined during the Depression era, and Hyten lost control of the business. He eventually went to work for Camark pottery as a salesman. Niloak pottery continued in business until 1947.

6" matte glazed squirrel planter, $75.00 – 100.00.
4¼" x 4¼" matte glazed frog planter, $75.00 – 100.00.

Mission Line produced in Arkansas.

10¼" vase, $400.00 – 500.00,
8½" vase, $300.00 – 400.00.
6½" vase, $250.00 – 300.00.
2½" x 4½" covered bowl, $400.00 – 450.00.

3¼" candlestick, $350.00 – 450.00.
7" bulbous vase, $1,000.00 – 1,200.00.
3½" flared vase, $200.00 – 250.00.
2¾" tapered vase, $150.00 – 175.00.

North Dakota School of Mines/ University of North Dakota Pottery (UND)

Grand Forks, North Dakota

The University of North Dakota School of Mines was established in 1898. A chemistry instructor, Ernie Babcock, surveyed the state's mineral resources during his summers and became the first director of the school. During the early years, emphasis was placed on utilitarian pottery and on the promotion of North Dakota clay.

In 1910, the school established a ceramics department, which was headed by Margaret Kelly Cable for 39 years. She was a potter from Minnesota who came from the Minneapolis Handicraft Guild, where the Arts and Crafts movement had been the dominant artistic influence. Cable, who had studied with artists such as Charles Binns and Frederick Hurten Rhead, initiated an emphasis on decorative art pottery which continued throughout her long tenure. She was by all accounts an excellent teacher.

Most of the North Dakota School of Mines artists were women. Several of the notable artists in addition to Margaret Kelly Cable were her sister Flora Cable Huckfield, Hildegarde Fried, Frieda L. Hammers, and Julia Edna Mattson. There is considerable information available about the contributions of the various UND artists. Mattson, for example, taught at UND for 39 years (1924 – 1963) and specialized in western designs. She used Native American designs and methods such as coil-built pottery.

Margaret Cable was known for her work with Native Americans at the Pine Ridge Sioux Reservation in South Dakota. She worked on the reservation for six months in 1937 and inspired others to develop Pine Ridge Pottery as a successful business (see Pine Ridge Pottery).

The pottery of the North Dakota School of Mines was always made of local clay. The styles of the work varied over the years. Many were simple shapes with solid-colored matte glazes. Some featured carved and painted borders or designs. The flora and fauna of the state were often depicted on the pottery. The wild prairie rose, the flickertail, and the meadowlark were examples of popular regional subject matter.

From 1913 to 1963 UND pottery was marked with a cobalt blue university seal. After that, pieces were marked only with the names of the artists. For years, there was almost no emphasis on the marketing and sales of UND pottery. In 1926 Margaret Cable pushed for more selling of the pottery, and it was then placed in some shops. Between 1938 and 1952 it was sold in all states and some other countries.

4" Bentonite squat vase with birds design, painted underglaze.
Signed by Longtime Instructor Julia Olson, $1,500.00 – 2,000.00.
3¾" vase dated 1935, signed by C. Ciland, $250.00 – 350.00.

5½" vase, signed by Cable, Flickertails and Wheat design, $1,200.00 – 1,500.00.
7¼" vase, cowboy design, signed by Julia Mattson, $3,000.00 – 3,500.00.
3½" vase, signed by Knudson, $700.00 – 800.00.

4" honey jar with lid, signed by Julia Mattson, $400.00 – 500.00.
3¾" vase, Flora Huckfield, covered wagons design, $500.00 – 600.00.
3¾" Prairie Rose vase, Flora Huckfield, $700.00 – 800.00.
5" pitcher, oxcart design, Margaret Cable, $800.00 – 900.00.

5" vase, 1941, signed
"D. Churchill," $350.00 – 450.00.
3½" flower bowl, signed "Red River,"
oxcart design, $800.00 – 900.00.
5" vase, signed "Huck,"
$450.00 – 550.00.
4" vase, signed "Passion Flower
Huck," $450.00 – 500.00.

4½" pin dish, $250.00 – 350.00.

5" jardiniere, $400.00 – 500.00.

2" x 4¼" bowl, $200.00 – 300.00.

7¼" vase, 1935, signed "M. Brenna,"
$400.00 – 500.00.

7" vase, dated 1912, $700.00 – 800.00.
9" vase, Matte Green, $1,000.00 – 1,200.00.
6½" teapot, 700.00 – 800.00.

2" curtain pull, Indian head design, $200.00 – 250.00.
2½" toothpick holder, $150.00 – 200.00.

12" lamp base, $500.00 – 600.00.
21" lamp base, signed "Flora Huckfield,"
$1,000.00 – 1,200.00.

2¼" x 4" covered pin dish, $300.00 – 350.00.

Bottom of the pin dish
showing the mark.

J. B. Owens Pottery
Zanesville, Ohio

J. B. Owens grew up in Muskingum County, Ohio, and became a salesman for a pottery in Roseville, Ohio. He then started his own pottery, incorporated as the J. B. Owens Pottery Company in 1891. Owens built a new plant and began manufacturing art pottery in 1896. His Utopian line was a high-glaze brown ware with underglaze slip painting, similar to other standard glaze lines of the time manufactured by Weller, Rookwood, and Roseville.

Although Owens manufactured art pottery for only a decade, during that time the company was known for employing highly talented artists and potters, introducing many lines, and publishing large catalogs. Some well-known potters and artists employed by Owens were Karl Langenbeck, John Lessell, and W. A. Long. Owens' art pottery won wide recognition, but in 1907 the company was closed. Soon thereafter, Owens changed direction to manufacturing commercial tile and the business was successful. However, the factory burned down in 1928 and his decision to rebuild at the beginning of the Depression proved to be a mistake. The company closed in 1929.

Two Matte Green jardinieres.
6½" jardiniere, $500.00 – 600.00.
8½" jardiniere, $800.00 – 900.00.

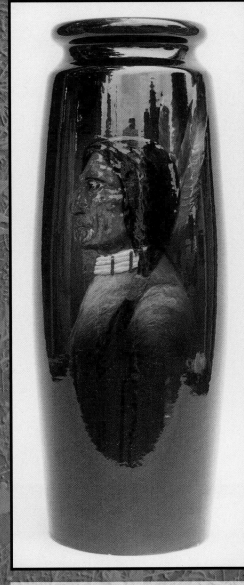

21" floor vase, $2,000.00 – 2,300.00.

Three nice vases.
10½" Art Vellum vase, c. 1905, $800.00 – 1,000.00.
16½" Mission line vase, c. 1903, $3,000.00 – 4,000.00.
13¼" Matte glazed vase, $500.00 – 600.00.

13" Opalescent Utopian line vase,
$1,000.00 – 1,200.00.

8" Lotus line vase, signed by Charles Chilcote, $2,500.00 – 3,000.00.

Peters & Reed Pottery/Zane Pottery

Zanesville, Ohio

John Peters and Adam Reed were former Weller pottery employees who decided to start their own pottery company in 1897. The Peters & Reed pottery was formally incorporated in 1901. Frank Ferrell, another Weller employee, joined the Peters & Reed pottery in 1905 as a designer. Ferrell introduced the popular Moss Aztec line.

Frank Ferrell left Peters & Reed to work for Roseville pottery in 1919. In 1920, the Peters & Reed Company was bought by Harry S. McClelland and Reed, and they changed the name to Zane Pottery Company. Reed died and McClelland continued to own and operate the Zane pottery for almost 20 years.

Peters & Reed pottery was primarily made of red clay from the Zanesville area. However, Zane pottery changed from red to white clay in 1926.

Peters & Reed art pottery is remarkable for its glazes and glaze treatments. The shapes used by Peters and Reed and Zane were often used repeatedly across many lines, with the glazes changed.

Some of many Peters & Reed and Zane lines include:

Decorated Ivory
Florentine
Landsun
Matte Green
Marbleized
Montene
Moss Aztec
Persian
Shadow Ware
Velvet Matte
Wilse Blue

Peters & Reed pottery was not marked. When the company's name was changed to Zane pottery, marking was done with an impressed mark or a rectangular Zane Ware ink stamp.

9" Cobalt Blue jardiniere, Persian line, $250.00 – 300.00.
6" Cobalt Blue vase, Persian line, $175.00 – 200.00.

Very rare 30" gnome with fish lawn ornament from the twentieth century, $7,000.00 – 8,000.00.

22" Moss Aztec umbrella stand,
$1,000.00 – 1,200.00.

19" sand jar, $1,000.00 – 1,100.00.

Moss Aztec collection.
5" hanging basket, $200.00 – 250.00.
6½" jardiniere, $300.00 – 350.00.
3½" hanging basket, $100.00 – 125.00.

Marbleized glaze collection.
10½" vase, $200.00 – 250.00.
2½" frog, $200.00 – 220.00.
12" vase, $250.00 – 300.00.
4½" creamer, $125.00 – 150.00.

27" marbleized glazed lamp, $400.00 – 500.00.

23" standard glazed lamp, $300.00 – 400.00.

6" decorated Landsun vase, $550.00 – 600.00.

7½" Montene vase, $175.00 – 200.00.

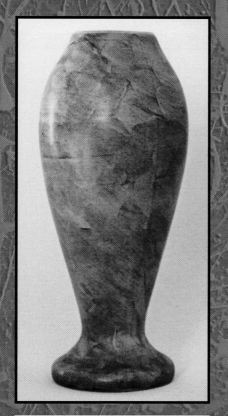

9" Landsun vase, $130.00 – 150.00.

9" marbleized glazed vase, $200.00 – 250.00.

12" Copper Montene glazed vase,
$500.00 – 600.00.

3" x 7" flower bowl, $150.00 – 200.00. 3" x 5" flower frog, $135.00 – 170.00.

Landsun vase collection.
5" vase, $190.00 – 250.00.
4" vase, $100.00 – 125.00.
5" vase, $180.00 – 235.00.
3½" vase, $110.00 – 135.00.
4" vase, $100.00 – 125.00.

Nice vase collection.
8" vase, $150.00 – 200.00.
10" vase, $175.00 – 225.00.
8" vase, $200.00 -$225.00.
12" vase, $225.00 – 250.00.

Flower bowl & flower frogs.
3" x 8" flower bowl, $150.00 – 200.00.
1" x 6" turtle flower frog, $125.00 – 150.00.
3" x 12" flower bowl, $200.00 – 250.00.
2" x 6" lily pad flower frog, $125.00 – 150.00.

Shadow Ware vase collection.
7" vase, $300.00 – 350.00.
8" vase, $325.00 – 375.00.
8" vase, $275.00 – 325.00.

Shadow Ware collection.
10" vase, $350.00 – 400.00.
8" bowl, $150.00 – 200.00.
9" vase, $275.00 – 325.00.

Decorated Ivory collection.
4" fan vase, $125.00 – 150.00.
9" vase, $175.00 – 225.00.
6" bud vase, $150.00 – 175.00.

The Wilse Blue collection.

4" jardiniere, $100.00 – 120.00.
6" bud vase, $110.00 – 120.00.
8" vase, $140.00 – 160.00.
9" vase, $125.00 – 150.00.
8" vase, $125.00 – 150.00.

Views of the bottoms of the vase
and candlestick.

10" twisted vase, $130.00 – 160.00.
9" vase, $140.00 – 170.00.
10" candlestick, $100.00 – 125.00.

7" candlesticks, $200.00 – 250.00 pair.
8" vase, $140.00 – 160.00.

Florentine collection.
9" vase, $150.00 – 200.00.
5½" jardiniere, $150.00 – 165.00.
6" jardiniere, $150.00 – 175.00.
5" vase, $120.00 – 150.00.
9" vase, $150.00 – 200.00.
7" vase, $140.00 – 160.00.

9" Moss Aztec wall pocket, $150.00 – 175.00.
8" Moss Aztec wall pocket, $175.00 – 200.00.

8" Wilse Blue wall pocket, $125.00 – 150.00.
6" Pink wall pocket, $130.00 – 150.00.
8" decorated Ivory wall pocket, $150.00 – 175.00.

4½" candleholder, $75.00 – 100.00.

Pewabic Pottery

Detroit, Michigan

Mary Chase Perry (Stratton) founded the Revelation Pottery with her neighbor, Horace James Caulkins, manufacturer of the Revelation kilns which were eventually used by many art pottery companies. Perry had attended art schools and was an accomplished china painter. Caulkins' kilns had originally been made for producing porcelain dental ware but he recognized their potential in the pottery business and enlisted Perry's help in marketing the kilns.

The pair experimented with pottery in a small studio and changed the pottery's name to Pewabic Pottery in 1903. The pottery moved to a new building in 1907. Perry and Caulkins started out making matte green pottery, but they expanded their color and glaze repertoire between 1904 and 1910.

The company's main focus soon turned to handmade tile. Pewabic received commissions for tile installations in institutions such as Detroit's main library, The Detroit Institute of Arts, and the Cathedral of St. John the Divine in New York City.

The Pewabic Pottery of Stratton and Caulkins was unusual in that it remained a small business with few employees. Horace Caulkins died in 1923. The company survived the Depression and continued to produce pottery until Mary Stratton's death in 1961 at the age of 94. After that, her former assistant operated the pottery until 1966, when ownership was transferred to Michigan State University, which operated the pottery as part of a continuing education program. Ownership was changed to the non-profit Pewabic Society in 1981. The pottery still operates as an institution with education, exhibition, museum and design, and fabrication programs. It is still housed in the building, now designated a National Historic Landmark, where Perry and Caulkins moved the Pewabic Pottery in 1907.

3" x 3" hand-painted tile, $200.00 – 300.00.

Pillin
Los Angeles, California

Polia Pillin emigrated to the United States from Poland in 1909, when she was 15 years old. She studied art in Chicago, while working in the garment industry. She and her husband William lived in New Mexico but then moved back to Chicago where Polin took some pottery classes at Hull House. The family moved to Los Angeles in 1948 and started a pottery studio. William Pillin worked with the clay and glazes while Polia Pillin specialized in the surface decoration, using a variety of surface techniques on her pottery. Her work, which is often adorned by portraiture, has been referred to as "art on pottery." Pillin was always a studio potter, so her output was limited and is now in high demand. She died in 1992.

13¼" decanter with stopper.
2¼" cups. $2,500.00 – 2,800.00 set.

6½" x 10¾" bowl, signed "Pillin,"
decorated with nine figures, $2,100.00 – 2,400.00.

3½" vase, $350.00 – 400.00.
7" vase, $500.00 – 600.00.

Pine Ridge Pottery
Pine Ridge Reservation, South Dakota

Pine Ridge Pottery was made on the Pine Ridge Reservation of the Oglala Lakota (Sioux) tribe, in western South Dakota. The tribe did not have a pottery tradition, as they were historically nomads. Looking to the successful example of the Southwestern Native Americans, the tribe became interested in developing Native American crafts as a means of self-help and economic development.

The tribe was assisted by Margaret Cable, director of ceramics at the University of North Dakota, who visited the Pine Ridge Reservation for six months in 1937 and encouraged the tribe in its pottery making. She taught classes and experimented with the local clay. Bruce Doyle, ceramics director at another reservation, was inspired by Cable to develop Pine Ridge pottery at the Pine Ridge Boarding School.

Doyle taught pottery classes to Native American adults and marketed the pottery around the state; he built up the business and stayed with it until 1942. One of Doyle's most skilled students had been Olive Cottier, and she and her two sisters, Ella Irving and Bernice Talbot, were largely responsible for keeping the pottery alive during the 1940s. They quit in 1953 when a new director was hired at the Pine Ridge Boarding School. In 1955, however, Ella Irving was able to purchase the pottery from the school and continue the business on her own. Her shop was destroyed by vandals in the 1980s and Pine Ridge pottery production came to an end.

The artists of Pine Ridge pottery signed their pieces with various names. Olive Cottier signed either "O. COTTIER" OR "RAMONA WOUNDED KNEE." Ella Irving used the names "WOODY" and "COX," her married names from two marriages, and also "IRVING." "NORA FIRETHUNDER" was the sisters' friend.

Pine Ridge pottery was made of local red clay. White clay used for the decoration was also from South Dakota. More decorated than plain pottery was made. The sgraffito carving technique was often used, and designs were often geometrical. Pieces were generally molded.

5" vase, signed "Firethunder," $200.00 – 300.00.
4½" vase, signed "O. Cottier," $200.00 – 250.00.
4½" vase, signed "O. Cottier," $225.00 – 275.00.

3" jug vase, signed "Woody," #338, $100.00 – 125.00.
3½" vase, signed "Woody," $150.00 – 200.00.
2½" flower bowl, signed "Ramona Wounded Knee," $200.00 – 250.00.

Red Wing
Red Wing, Minnesota

The Red Wing Stoneware Company began in 1878 in Red Wing, Minnesota, and merged with Minnesota Stoneware Company in 1906 to become the Red Wing Union Stoneware Company. In 1936 it became Red Wing Potteries, Inc., and the company endured until 1967 when it had labor problems and also difficulty in competing with foreign imports.

The company made pottery starting in the 1920s. They made artware, but also kitchenware, flowerpots, stoneware, and lamps. The company began making dinnerware successfully during the 1930s. They made over 90 patterns of dinnerware.

Early Red Wing pottery was a kind of molded stoneware called Brushed Ware, which was stained in shades of green or tan; the stain was then partially brushed off. The company began making glazed art pottery in 1929 with its new tunnel kiln.

From about 1932 to 1937, Red Wing made pottery for George RumRill, a distributor who sold the pottery under the RumRill name.

Red Wing's Glazed Ware, produced into the early 1930s, was glossy or semi-matte. The Nokomis glaze, a semi-matte glaze, is now highly collectible. A variety of shapes and designs were offered, and the pieces were molded.

8" Nokomis vase, $350.00 – 450.00.

Athenian group collection.
RumRill by Red Wing vases.
9½" vase, $600.00 – 800.00.
10½" vase, $1,000.00 – 1,600.00.
11½" vase, $1,100.00 – 1,300.00.

9½" double-handled vase, $125.00 – 150.00.
12" double-handled vase, $150.00 – 175.00.

5" x 8¾" flower bowl,
nice Cobalt Blue interior, $100.00 – 150.00.

Robinson-Ransbottom Pottery Company (RRP)

Roseville, Ohio

In 1920, the Ransbottom Brothers Pottery of Roseville, Ohio, merged with Robinson Clay Products of Akron, Ohio, to form the new Robinson-Ransbottom Pottery Company (often referred to as RRP). Prior to 1920 the Ransbottom Brothers had manufactured utilitarian stoneware, bricks, and stoneware jars. After 1920, as the Robinson-Ransbottom Pottery Company, more artistic pieces were produced, some of which were signed by the artists who decorated them. The company stayed in business until 2005. Unlike many of the Ohio potteries, the RRP Company's plant was never destroyed by fire, which may partly account for its longevity.

32" jardiniere & pedestal, $1,600.00 – 1,800.00.
26" tankard-shaped floor vase, $1,400.00 – 1,500.00.
Both pieces were produced in the 1920s.

Billboard on the highway to Roseville, Ohio, 2004.

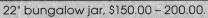
22" bungalow jar, $150.00 – 200.00.

14" floor vase, $125.00 – 150.00.

15" ribbed floor vase
Penny the chihuahua loves it!
$150.00 – 200.00.

Early 24" floor vase,
hand-painted underglaze, $1,200.00 – 1,500.00.

Early 21" floor vase,
hand-painted underglaze,
$600.00 – 700.00.

22" floor vase, early 1920s,
$1,000.00 – 2,000.00.

19" floor vase, dated 6-20-90,
painted by Rick Wisecarver, $700.00 – 800.00.

18" oil jar, 1940s, signed "Willard Pace"
(he was in charge of art dept.), $600.00 – 700.00.
27" floor vase, 1930s, $1,200.00 – 1,400.00.

Dorothy Archer signed vases.
11" vase, $200.00 – 225.00.
9" vase, $175.00 – 200.00.
27" floor vase, $500.00 – 600.00.

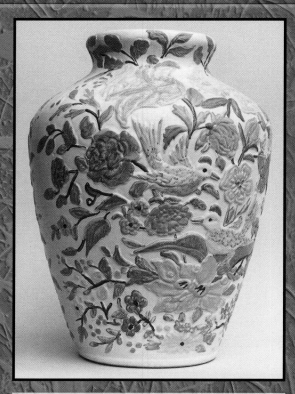

21" floor vase, signed "Dorothy Archer,"
$600.00 – 750.00.

Two floor vases.
18", $200.00 – 250.00.
14", $100.00 – 150.00.

14" floor vase, signed "Dorothy Archer,"
$200.00 – 250.00.

13" floor vase, $100.00 – 120.00.
10" jardiniere, $75.00 – 100.00.

Apple pattern oil jar, $150.00 – 200.00.

12" falcon, $350.00 – 400.00.

12" decorated oil jar, $100.00 – 150.00.

Rookwood Pottery
Cincinnati, Ohio

Maria Longworth Nichols founded the Rookwood Pottery of Cincinnati, Ohio, in 1880. She had earlier taken up china painting, a popular hobby of American women of that time, and that led to an interest in pottery and glazes. Rookwood Pottery, which was to become the preeminent American Art pottery company, began by making toilet seats, pitchers, and gray stoneware. During the early years, the pottery was not financially successful but was supported by Nichols' wealthy family. In 1883, William Watts Taylor became a partner and administrator and began to improve the business operations of the pottery. Mrs. Nichols' husband died in 1885, and in 1886 she married Bellamy Storer.

In 1889, Rookwood won a gold medal at the Universal Exposition in Paris, and the company began to be profitable. It was the beginning of Rookwood's most successful period. Maria Longworth Nichols Storer retired from the pottery in 1890 and William Watts Taylor became the president. Taylor died in 1913 and was succeeded by Joseph Henry Gest, who remained president until 1934. The pottery survived the WWI and Depression years. The following years were marked by changes of ownership and operation until the pottery closed in 1967.

Rookwood is widely regarded as one of the most outstanding American art pottery companies. The company's standards were high, and the quality was consistent. Rookwood pottery was cast from molds. Some pieces were plain; others were incised or decorated. There were a variety of products. The works were marked with the date of manufacture, and the hand-decorated pieces were often signed or monogrammed by the decorators. The company won awards at national and international expositions.

Rookwood employed numerous outstanding artists over the years. One of the most famous was Kataro Shirayamadani, who worked at the pottery for 54 years. Another was Artus Van Briggle, who left Rookwood to start his own company in Colorado. Many of the Rookwood artists were women, such as Louise Abel and Sarah Sax.

Rookwood's Standard Glaze line, introduced in 1884, was extremely popular. The company introduced matte glazes in 1901. The Rookwood Vellum glaze was introduced in 1904 and had a soft hazy appearance reminiscent of Impressionist paintings. The Matte Vellum was transparent enough to be used over colored slip decoration. Framed vellum-glazed wall plaques (tiles) became a popular and beautiful Rookwood product.

The Cincinnati Art Museum has a large Rookwood collection, as does the National Museum of History and Technology (Smithsonian Institution).

6" x 7" elephant bookends, dated 1929, #2444C, $1,600.00 – 2,100.00 for the pair.

34" draped nude garden statue, signed "W. P. McDonald," produced in the twentieth century, too rare to price.

W. P. McDonald signature on the base.

12" x 12" base of statue, notice the mark.

Three tiles that measure 12" x 13" each, 1920s, $14,000.00 – 16,000.00, original frame.

10¾" x 8¾" tile, in original frame,
by Frederick Rothenbusch,
dated 1912, $8,000.00 – 10,000.00.

11" x 9" tile in original frame,
by Frederick Rothenbusch,
1916, $10,000.00 – 12,000.00.

5" x 9" tile in original frame, by Lenore Asbury, 1927, $6,000.00 – 7,000.00.

7½" x 4" tile in original frame, by Carl Schmidt, 1911, $3,000.00 – 4,000.00.

14" x 11" tile in original frame, by Frederick Rothenbusch, $12,000.00 – 14,000.00.

Hand-painted vases by Edward Diers,
11½" vase, 1916, $3,500.00 – 4,500.00.
11" vase, 1923, rare scene, $10,000.00 – 12,000.00.
9" vase, 1922, rare scene, $3,500.00 – 4,500.00.

Hand-painted vases.
14" vase, by Elizabeth Lincoln, 1922, $3,800.00 – 4,200.00.
7" vase, by Louise Abel, 1926, $2,500.00 – 2,700.00.
12" vase, by Lorinda Epply, 1916, $3,600.00 – 3,800.00.

8½" vase, by Harriet Wilcox, early matte, 1903, $9,000.00 – 12,000.00.
12" vase, by C. S. Todd, early matte, 1917, $6,000.00 – 8,000.00.
14" vase, by C. S. Todd, early matte, 1912, $6,000.00 – 8,000.00.

5" ginger jar, 1924, $1,500.00 – 2,000.00.
9¼" vase, 1927, $2,000.00 – 2,500.00.
6" vase, 1925, $800.00 – 1,000.00.
All by Elizabeth Lincoln.

5" x 5" dog bookends, 1937, $600.00 – 700.00.
4" x 3" rook paperweight, 1918, $550.00 – 650.00.
3" x 3" frog ash receiver, 1931, $300.00 – 400.00.

5½" x 5" rook bookends, 1924, $600.00 – 700.00.
7¼" x 5½" parrot bookends, 1927, $4,000.00 – 5,000.00.
6¼" x 4" owl bookends, 1940, $350.00 – 450.00.

5¼" beggar mug, twentieth century,
by Artus Van Briggle, $1,300.00 – 1,500.00.
7¾" covered pitcher, by Artus Van Briggle,
1819, $2,000.00 – 2,300.00.
5¼" handled vase, by Leona Van Briggle,
1900, $400.00 – 600.00.

7" vase, 1940,
by Margaret McDonald, $1,200.00 – 1,300.00.

9½" vase, by Kataro Shirayamadani, 1930, $3,200.00 – 3,500.00.
15" vase, by Fredrick Rothenbusch, 1923, $2,500.00 – 3,000.00.

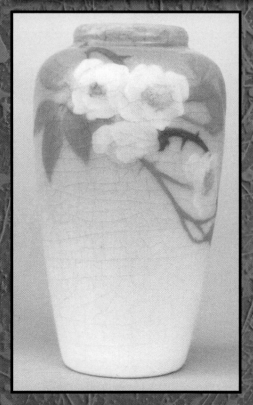

4½" vase, 1911, $300.00 – 400.00.
7" three-handled vase, 1912, $600.00 – 700.00.

4½" vase, by Elizabeth Lincoln, 1906, $800.00 – 900.00.

Pair 4½" x 7" bookends, designed by Louise Abel, 1935, $2,500.00 – 3,000.00.

Two nice vases.
5" vase, 1915, $500.00 – 600.00.
4½" vase, 1922, $450.00 – 550.00.

2½" x 6", match holder & striker, 1920, $800.00 – 900.00.

5¼" Rooster paperweight, 1946, $450.00 – 500.00.

3" x 4" vase, by Shirayamadani, dated 1899, $1,000.00 – 1,200.00.

Rosemeade Pottery
Wahpeton, North Dakota

Rosemeade pottery was the inspiration of Laura Taylor, a rural North Dakota teacher in a one-room schoolhouse whose interest in art awakened when she did art projects with her students. Taylor went back to school to study art and ceramics and exhibited her ceramic tile at the North Dakota building at the 1934 Chicago World's Fair. Two years later, she became state superintendent of the Works Progress Administration Federal Clay Project in Dickinson, North Dakota, and in 1939 she demonstrated pottery making at the New York World's Fair. At the fair, she met North Dakota businessman Robert Hughes, who proposed they start a pottery company. The Wahpeton Pottery Company was founded in 1940. In 1943, Hughes and Taylor were married.

In 1953 Wahpeton Pottery Company changed its name to Rosemeade Potteries. Rosemeade was the name of the product and it was confusing to have the two names. In 1956 the new production manager, Joe McLaughlin, began importing white clay from Kentucky for Rosemeade manufacture; it dried more quickly, shrank less, and produced a whiter pottery. North Dakota clay was also still used.

Rosemeade pottery was successful from the beginning. Laura Taylor was highly regarded as a technician and artist. She created most Rosemeade designs herself but some designs, particularly those of horses and western scenes, were created by Vera Gethman. Employees were trained in all phases of the manufacture of pottery and their jobs were rotated for variety.

Rosemeade pottery was usually made of buff-colored clay and cast in molds made from Laura Taylor's original clay models. Subject matter often reflects North Dakota's monuments, natural landscape, and animals. Salt and pepper shakers were popular, as were animal figurines, planters and vases. Some pieces were made as advertising items.

Rosemeade pottery closed in 1964; Laura Taylor had died of cancer in 1959, minimum wage had risen, and there was competition from Asian imitations of Rosemeade pottery which sold for much less than the originals.

3½" salt & pepper shakers, $65.00– 85.00 each.

Back view.

3½" monkey figurine, $150.00 – 200.00.

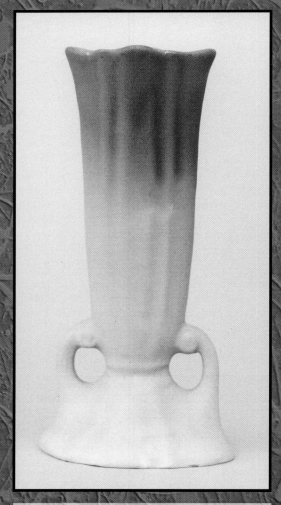

7½" vase, $100.00 – 125.00.

6" vase, $100.00 – 150.00.
3¼" vase, $50.00 – 75.00.

Roseville Pottery
Roseville and Zanesville, Ohio

The Roseville Pottery Company, Inc., was one of the most prominent, prolific, and popular of all American potteries. George F. Young started the company in 1891, in Roseville, Ohio, and became general manager when the company was incorporated in 1892. Several plants were acquired, but after 1917 all Roseville pottery was made in Zanesville. Roseville began making art pottery around 1900.

Early Roseville art pottery, named Rozane, was hand-decorated, with dark standard glaze, and was comparable in appearance to contemporary lines made by Weller and Rookwood. Later lines using the Rozane mark were more diverse. The company produced numerous art pottery lines, many with a particular flower's name such as Wisteria, Sunflower, or Columbine. Many famous designers worked at Roseville, such as Harry and Frederick Hurten Rhead, Frank Ferrell, and John J. Herold. Rhead designed the famous Della Robbia line, characterized by an unusual carving technique. Ferrell was known for designing the company's popular Pine Cone line (1931). The decorators and designers often worked at other potteries before or after working for Roseville.

Individual artist decorating was discontinued at Roseville by 1920. There was more demand for matte rather than glossy finish, and for molded designs.

Russell T. Young succeeded his father as general manager of Roseville in 1917, and when he died in 1931 his mother, Anna M. Young took that position and kept the business going through the Depression. In fact, many of Roseville's most popular lines were released during the 1930s.

Current collectors must be aware of a flood of Roseville imitations coming from Asia. Unfortunately, the imitations are becoming more accurate and hard to identify.

19" pre-1916 Matte Green umbrella stand, $1,000.00 – 1,200.00.
20" Vista line umbrella stand, $2,500.00 – 3,000.00.

Three early Roseville vases.
11" Crystalis vase, $2,000.00 – 2,500.00.
11" Egypto vase, $1,800.00 – 2,100.00.
10½" Rozane Fudji vase, $3,100.00 – 3,600.00.

Three Vista vases.
18" vase, $1,800.00 – 2,200.00.
18" vase, $2,000.00 – 2,300.00.
10" vase, $700.00 – 800.00.

Vista line.
10" vase, $750.00 – 850.00.
7" jardiniere, $650.00 – 750.00.

Carnelian II vases.
8" vase, $600.00 – 800.00.
19" vase, $4,000.00 – 5,000.00.
8" vase, $500.00 – 700.00.

Three Carnelian vases.
10" vase, $800.00 – 900.00.
7" vase, $400.00 – 450.00.
5" vase, $300.00 – 350.00.

5" x 14" Carnelian console bowl.
With 3½" flower arranger, $700.00 – 800.00 set.

Pair of Carnelian candleholders,
2" x 3½", $200.00 – 250.00.

27½" jardiniere & pedestal,
signed by Harry Rhead,
$5,200.00 – 5,500.00.

21½" Rozane ware floor vase,
signed by Arthur Williams,
$12,000.00 – 14,000.00.

Signature on Rozane vase.

10" vase, $400.00 – 500.00.
8" vase, $300.00 – 400.00.

13" Rozane Ware vase,
$600.00 – 700.00.

4" Matte Green vase, $175.00 – 225.00.
4½" jardiniere, $275.00 – 325.00.
3½" x 8½" Chloron vase, $800.00 – 900.00.

3½" x 5½" flower bowl, $150.00 – 200.00.

4" x 6" Matte Green
hanging basket, $300.00 – 400.00.

10" Victorian art pottery vase, $800.00 – 1,000.00.
8½" Imperial II vase, $700.00 – 800.00.

Wall pocket collection.
8" x 12" Egypto, $3,500.00 – 4,000.00.
7" x 6½" Imperial II & Earlam.
Each, $950.00 – 1,100.00.
8" x 8" Baneda, $4,000.00 – 4,500.00.

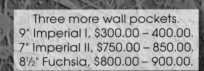

Three more wall pockets.
9" Imperial I, $300.00 – 400.00.
7" Imperial II, $750.00 – 850.00.
8½" Fuchsia, $800.00 – 900.00.

Three more wall pockets.
8½" Velmoss, $2,500.00 – 3,000.00.
8½" Poppy, $1,000.00 – 1,200.00.
9½" Rosecraft panel, $450.00 – 550.00.

7" Good Night Creamware
chamberstick, $500.00 – 600.00.
26" Majolica line, 1900, $3,000.00 – 3,500.00.
11" Creamware Gibson Girl
vase, $2,000.00 – 2,200.00.

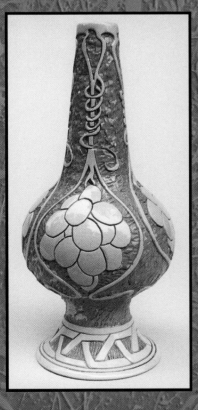

Della Robbia vase,
$1,500.00 – 2,000.00.

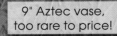

9" Aztec vase,
too rare to price!

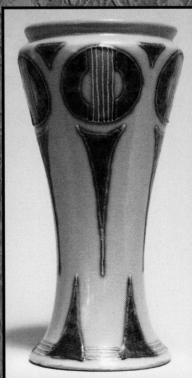

Sunflower collection.
29" jardiniere & pedestal, $5,500.00 – 6,500.00.
9½" vase, $1,600.00 – 1,900.00.
8" vase, $1,800.00 – 2,000.00.
5" hanging basket, $1,300.00 – 1,400.00.

29" Blackberry jardiniere &
pedestal, $4,000.00 – 5,000.00.

28" Wisteria jardiniere & pedestal, $4,000.00 – 5,500.00.

3" x 8½" Della Robbia vase, $7,000.00 – 8,000.00.
7½" Tourist vase, $2,000.00 – 2,500.00.
5" tumbler, signed by Frederick Rhead,
too rare to price.

Wall pocket collection.
8½" Rosecraft Hexagon Line, $625.00 – 725.00.
7½" Rosecraft Panel Nude, $800.00 – 900.00.
9" Rosecraft Vintage, $500.00 – 650.00.
8½" Morning Glory, $2,000.00 – 2,300.00.
9" Vista, $1,200.00 – 1,500.00.
10" Ceramic design, $500.00 – 600.00.

Pre-1916 Matte Green.
4" x 6½" hanging basket, $150.00 – 200.00.
4½" x 5½" hexagonal bowl, $350.00 – 450.00.
4¼" x 5" hanging basket, $200.00 – 250.00.

Poppy Line collection.
6" jardiniere, $200.00 – 250.00.
18" ewer vase, $700.00 – 800.00.
9" vase, $450.00 – 550.00.
6" vase, $250.00 – 350.00.

4½" Sunflower bowl, $600.00 – 700.00.
6" Blackberry vase, $700.00 – 800.00.
6" Baneda vase, $700.00 – 800.00.

4" x 8" Poppy jardiniere, $300.00 – 350.00.
6½" Columbine vase, $200.00 – 250.00.
7½" Clemana vase, $500.00 – 600.00.

Tourmaline line collection.
7" vase, $250.00 – 300.00.
9" vase, $300.00 – 400.00.
5" vase, $200.00 – 300.00.

Blackberry collection.
4" jardiniere, $350.00 – 450.00.
6" vase, $750.00 – 850.00.
5" vase, $650.00 – 750.00.

Fuchsia line collection.
12" vase, $600.00 – 700.00.
3½" x 14½" flower bowl,
$500.00 – 600.00.
6" vase, $200.00 – 300.00.

Pine Cone collection.
10½" vase, $600.00 – 700.00.
8" jardiniere, $800.00 – 900.00.
8" vase, $500.00 – 600.00.

19" Pine Cone floor vase, $2,100.00 – 2,600.00.

19" White Rose floor vase, $1,600.00 – 1,800.00.

Gardenia collection.
2½" x 6" bowl, $125.00 – 150.00.
5" bowl, $135.00 – 160.00.

11" Gardenia lamp, $200.00 – 250.00.

10½" jardiniere, Rozane, 1917, $400.00 – 475.00.

1917 Rozane collection.
6½" vase, $175.00 – 200.00.
6½" x 9½" compote, $200.00 – 250.00.
2¼" vase, $175.00 – 200.00.

Orian line collection.
7" vase, $300.00 – 350.00.
7" vase, $400.00 – 500.00.
7" vase, $300.00 – 350.00.

25" Mongol lamp, $1,000.00 – 1,200.00.

5½" x 7" scarab jardiniere, $350.00 – 450.00.

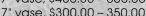

Dogwood II jardinieres.
7", $200.00 – 250.00.
6", $150.00 – 200.00.

15" Mostique floor vase, $600.00 – 800.00.
12½" Dogwood I vase, $500.00 – 600.00.

Mock Orange line
jardiniere & pedestal, $1,800.00 – 2,000.00.

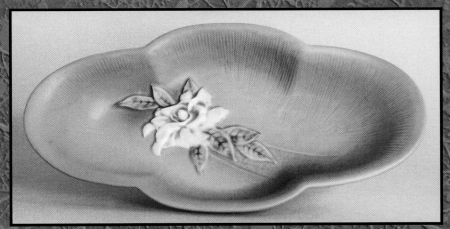

15" Gardenia tray, $225.00 – 275.00.

12½" Crystal Green vase,
$300.00 – 400.00.

10" Futura jardiniere, $900.00 – 1,000.00.

10" Bleeding Heart jardiniere, $900.00 – 1,000.00.

White Rose collection.
7" vase, $150.00 – 200.00.
8" vase, $175.00 – 250.00.
7" vase, $125.00 – 150.00.

Moss line collection.
3" x 6" bowl, $150.00 – 175.00.
5" vase, $165.00 – 200.00.

Dahlrose collection.
3½" x 10" bowl, $165,00 – 185.00.
7" jardiniere, $200.00 – 250.00.
4½" x 10½" flower bowl, $175.00 -$200,00.

Pre-1916 Dutch Creamware.
5" stein, $125.00 – 150.00 each.
11½" tankard, $350.00 – 400.00.

Pre-1916 Donatella tea set.
4" covered sugar,
4½" teapot,
3" creamer. $700.00 – 800.00 set.

Early 3" x 5" vase, $75.00 – 100.00.

8" Freesia jar, $450.00 – 550.00.

Rushmore/Colony Town
Keystone, South Dakota

The Rushmore pottery was established by Ivan Houser and W. S. Tallman in 1933 in Keystone, South Dakota. Houser, a sculptor and artist from Oregon, was an assistant to Gutzon Borglum, creator of the Mount Rushmore memorial. Tallman was also a sculptor and artist who became superintendent in charge of all work on Mount Rushmore. While driving in South Dakota, Houser spotted a clay deposit near the highway, experimented with it, and purchased land for use in producing pottery. He and Tallman made pottery and their wives, Mildred Houser and Peggy Tallman, sold it to Mount Rushmore tourists during the summers. Tallman sold his share of Rushmore pottery to Houser in 1940, and Houser sold the pottery in 1942 before moving back to Oregon after his mother's death.

In Aurora, Oregon, Houser founded the Colony Town Pottery and operated it for three years. The pottery was not very successful. Houser himself remained active as a professor at Lewis and Clark College in Portland, Oregon, for 16 years.

Rushmore pottery was almost all hand-thrown, but during the later years some inexpensive molded items were made. The native clay was excellent and did not require additives. Houser created his own glazes, most famously his Orange Uranium glaze, which was discontinued during World War II. In general, Rushmore pottery is undecorated, its beauty relying on shape and glaze.

7½" Rushmore vase, $200.00 – 250.00.
4½" Rushmore vase, $125.00 – 150.00.
6" Colony Town vase, $75.00 – 100.00.
7½" Colony Town vase, monkey head handles, $100.00 – 125.00.

Taylor Tilery
Santa Monica, California

The Taylor Tilery was part of the Santa Monica Brick Company, Santa Monica, California. The tilery was in business from about 1934 to 1938. Taylor Tilery tiles were made of red clay decorated with bright glazes. Some of the Taylor Tilery tiles featured California motifs, flora and fauna, while others had bright, Moorish designs. The tiles were often used in tables and stairways. Bill Handley, who had previously worked at Malibu potteries, was an important designer at Taylor Tilery. Under his influence, the tilery began producing some tiles with a finer black-line painting style.

16½" square tile lamp table, $1,000.00 – 1,200.00.

12" x 24" tile table top.
Tiles are 5¾" each, $800.00 – 1,000.00.

12" x 18" tile lamp table, $2,000.00 – 2,500.00.

TECO

Terra Cotta, Illinois

William D. Gates was an attorney who started a tile company in 1879 in Terra Cotta, Illinois. Until 1887, the factory made terra cotta bricks for architectural purposes, pottery, and utilitarian ceramics. The factory was partially destroyed in 1887 and rebuilt. Then the company was incorporated and renamed the American Terra Cotta and Ceramic Company, also referred to as Gates Pottery. The company is most famous for its TECO line of art pottery. The company declined during the 1920s and closed shortly after the stock market crash.

The TECO line (the name came from the first two letters of terra and cotta) debuted in 1901. The company employed numerous artists and architects, including Frank Lloyd Wright. William Gates, the company's founder, designed many of the TECO pieces.

TECO pottery is almost always matte green. However, other glazes were used. The majority of early TECO pieces were vases, but garden pottery, tableware, and tiles were also made. The vases were cast in molds, and mass-produced. Subject matter, molded into the design, often featured leaves or plants. The pottery was seldom decorated.

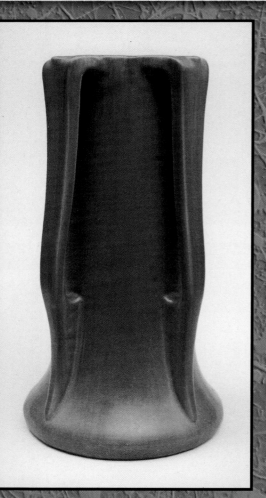

18" floor vase,
wonderful Arts & Crafts
shape, $12,000.00 – 15,000.00.

11" vase, $2,000.00 – 2,500.00.
3¾" ewer, $300.00 – 400.00.
4½" vase, Lemon Peel glaze, $450.00 – 550.00.

Van Briggle Pottery
Colorado Springs, Colorado

Artus Van Briggle was born in Felicity, Ohio, in 1869 and moved to Cincinnati as a young man to study art. He worked at the Avon Pottery and later at the Rookwood Pottery Company. Van Briggle was a prominent designer at Rookwood, and the company paid for his further art studies in Paris and Italy. The founder of Rookwood, Maria Storer, supported Van Briggle as he worked to rediscover the dead glazes of ancient Ming Dynasty pottery.

Van Briggle suffered from tuberculosis and moved to Colorado in 1899 with the belief that the climate would be good for his health. He began exploring the area and found deposits of clay and minerals for his use. Once he had developed glazes and designs and had found suitable Colorado clays, he started his pottery in 1901, with support from Maria Storer. The Van Briggle Pottery Company was formally established in 1902 as a stock company.

In the same year, 1902, Artus Van Briggle married his artist fiancée, Anne Lawrence Gregory. She had also been a decorator at Rookwood. Artus Van Briggle died in 1904, and Anne Van Briggle became president of the company. She oversaw the opening of a new plant, the Van Briggle Memorial Pottery, in 1908. In 1912, she sold her interest in the company and was no longer involved in the company's management.

The ensuing years included several changes of ownership, financial hardships and periodic brief closures, and a flood in 1935 that destroyed pottery molds and documents.

Early Van Briggle pottery is notable for its sculptural quality and beautiful matte glazes. Flora and fauna are popular subject matter. Two of the most famous Van Briggle designs are the "Lorelei" vase, with a woman wrapped around and blended into the top of a vase, and "Despondency," a vase with a human figure curled up and blended into the top of the vase. Dating Van Briggle pottery is difficult. Pieces made between 1901 and 1907 were dated. Artus and Anne Van Briggle did not sign their work. Early pieces were marked with a "Double A" (for Artus and Anne) trademark.

Van Briggle is one of the few American art pottery companies to have survived to this day.

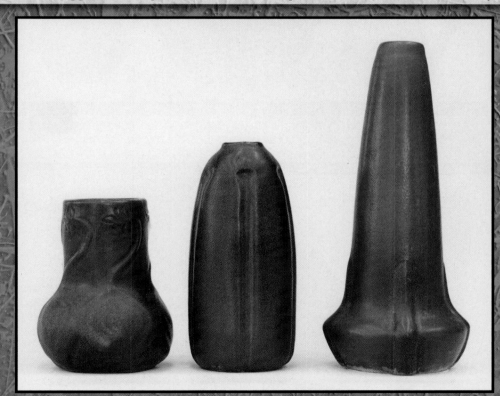

Three 1920s vases.
4¼", $300.00 – 400.00.
5¾", $500.00 – 600.00.
8", $650.00 – 750.00.

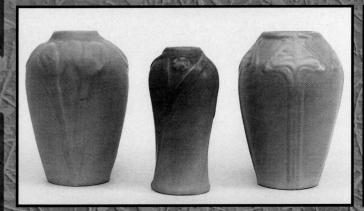

5¾" Tulip vase, 1911, $500.00 – 600.00.
5" vase, 1911, $450.00 – 550.00.
5½" Arrow vase, 1905, $700.00 – 800.00.

4¼" Matte Green vase, 1905, $750.00 – 850.00.
7½" Persian Rose vase, 1920, $350.00 – 450.00.
4½" Matte Green mug, 1904, $1,100.00 – 1,300.00.

3½" Persian Rose chamberstick, 1916, $300.00 – 400.00.
3" Acorn squat vase, 1920s, $250.00 – 300.00.
5" Persian Rose vase, 1919, $400.00 – 500.00.

4½" bottle vase from 1905, $700.00 – 800.00.
7¾" deep Dark Blue vase, 1920, $300.00 – 350.00.
6" Seafoam Green vase, 1920, $350.00 – 400.00.

10¼" double-handled vase, 1920s, $350.00 – 450.00.
12" Ming Blue vase, 1920s, $400.00 – 550.00.
4½" Persian Rose vase, 1918, $400.00 – 500.00.

8" double-handled vase, 1917, $350.00 – 450.00,
12" candlestick lamp base, 1911, $350.00 – 450.00.
10½" double-handled vase, 1911, $500.00 – 600.00.

Three small vases.
3¾", $150.00 – 200.00.
3⅓", $275.00 – 300.00.
3¾", $150.00 – 200.00.

4¼" bear paperweight, $450.00 – 500.00.
7" bear bookend, $200.00 – 300.00.

Bottom of bear paperweight, marked
"VBPCo," Van Briggle Pottery Co.

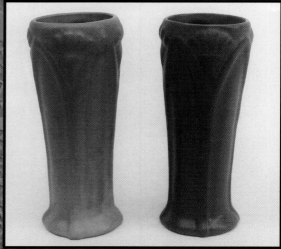

Persian Rose collection.
9" vase, 1920, $800.00 – 900.00.
12" vase, 1930, $450.00 – 500.00.
6" x 10" bowl / vase, 1917, nice! $600.00 – 800.00.

7¼" Dark Ming Blue vase, 1920, $225.00 – 300.00.
7¼" Dark Persian Rose vase, 1920, $225.00 – 300.00.

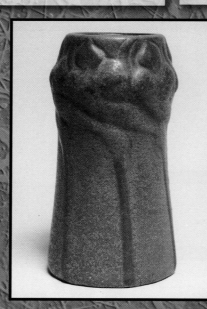

14½" vase, $500.00 – 600.00.
17½" vase, $400.00 – 425.00.

6½" vase, 1907, $1,000.00 – 1,300.00.

3½" vase, 1903, signed "Artus Van Briggle," $1,500.00 – 2,000.00.

2¼" vase, 1930s, $150.00 – 200.00.
3" vase, 1940s, $125.00 – 160.00.

16" Despondency vase, 1990s, $500.00 – 600.00.

14" x 12½" x 8½" Siren of the Sea bowl,
6¼" x 5½" flower frog, $1,400.00 – 1,600.00.

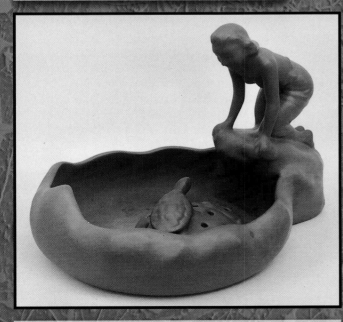

Lady of the Lake flower bowl &
flower frog, 10" tall, $500.00 – 600.00.

Water Nymph, flower bowl &
flower frog, 9¾", $500.00 – 600.00.

Weller Pottery

Zanesville, Ohio

Weller pottery is closely identified with its founder, Sam Weller, who opened the company around 1872, when he was 21 years old, in Fultonham, Ohio. At first it was nothing more than a simple cabin on a farm where he and one assistant dug clay and made flowerpots by hand to sell in Zanesville.

Weller Pottery expanded, and by 1882 the company was relocated to Zanesville. Sam Weller acquired the Lonhuda pottery of Steubenville in 1895 and its former owner, W. A. Long, came to work for Weller. Lonhuda Ware was then made at Weller Pottery, but the name of the line was changed to Louwelsa when W. A. Long left Weller in 1896. The Louwelsa line is characterized by a high-gloss glaze, often green or brown, similar to Rookwood's standard glaze. Underglaze decoration typically features flowers, dogs, Native Americans, and famous men. The line was an enormous success for Weller.

Weller Pottery often used one shape for several lines. The company manufactured hand-decorated pottery in its earlier years, often artist-signed. Sam Weller was successful in attracting the services of numerous superb artists, among them Jacques Sicard, Frederick Hurten Rhead, and John Lessell. After World War I, Weller and its competitors began making more commercial and mass-produced products.

Weller bought the Zanesville Art Pottery in 1920. It became Weller Plant #3, the Ceramic Avenue plant. The head of the decorating department was John Lessell.

Sam Weller died in 1925 and a nephew became president of the pottery. The company survived the Depression but had to downsize. It revived somewhat during World War II, but eventually changed hands and closed permanently in 1948.

Selected Weller Lines:

Weller produced numerous lines of pottery between 1895 and 1945. In general, pottery from the early period is most valuable.

One especially notable line was Sicardo, distinctive with its iridescent metallic glaze of mixed colors like magenta and gold, and both free-form and naturalistic designs. Sicardo was made between 1902 and 1907 when Jacques Sicard and his assistant, Henri Gellie, came from France to work for Weller. Sicard insisted on working in secrecy so that no one, including Sam Weller, could learn his formula for Sicardo. Sicard himself had learned the process as an employee of Clement Massier in France. Massier's iridescent pottery was known as Reflets Metalliques.

Weller's Matte Green pottery, introduced in 1905, is a dark green matte pottery with raised designs of leaves or other natural designs. Many companies were manufacturing similar lines around the same time in imitation of Grueby's handmade matte green pottery. Matte Green is still very popular and highly collectible.

Dickens Ware was the name for three lines produced between 1897 and 1910. The first line resembled Louwelsa. The second line had sgraffito (incised) decorations of scenes from Dickens and other subject matter. The third and latest line of Dickens Ware was created by noted designer Frederick Hurten Rhead.

Yet another outstanding early Weller line was Eocean, characterized by underglaze slip decoration, and flora and fauna subject matter, with a light glossy shaded background.

There were several types of the Hudson line. All were semi-matte. Most have shaded backgrounds and feature either floral or scenic backgrounds. The pieces are characterized by underglaze, hand-painted decoration, and were usually signed by the artist.

The Woodcraft line was introduced in 1917. This pottery's surface looks like tree bark and the pieces are decorated with forest creatures and plants.

Coppertone, another line popular with collectors, was produced during the late 1920s and is marked by a bright green gloss over brown glaze on shapes featuring frogs, fish, and other forms from nature.

Four Hudson vases.
7" Perfecto vase, $1,500.00 – 1,800.00.
10½", signed by Pillsbury, $1,100.00 – 1,300.00.
15½", signed by Sarah McLaughlin, $4,000.00 – 4,200.00.
10½", signed by Dorothy England, $900.00 – 1,000.00.

Three Hudson vases.
13" blue vase, $2,000.00 – 2,250.00.
9½", signed by Eugene Roberts, $3,500.00 – 4,000.00.
13½", signed by Gitter, $3,000.00 – 3,500.00.

Coppertone collection.

8" fish, $4,000.00 – 5,000.00.
17" x 3" console bowl, $1,500.00 – 2,000.00.
6" turtle figurine, $500.00 – 600.00.
2" frog figurine, $300.00 – 350.00.

4" frog on lotus flower, $400.00 – 500.00.

9" bud vase with climbing frog, $1,000.00 – 1,200.00.
8" vase with frog handles, $1,600.00 – 1,800.00.
8½" double fish bud vase, $4,000.00 – 5,000.00.

22" Sicard floor vase, $12,000.00 – 15,000.00.
6" vase made by Clement Massier. Clement Massier
Studio is where Sicard studied before coming to the U.S.
and working for Weller pottery. Too rare to price.
4¾" Sicard vase, $1,000.00 – 1,200.00.

31" Matte Green jardiniere & pedestal,
11" jardiniere, 21½" pedestal,
$1,800.00 – 2,200.00.

Two 7" Lasa vases, left and right, $600.00 – 700.00 each.
Center 7" vase with handles was produced by Owen China of Minerva, Ohio,
in 1906 and was part of the Swastika Keramos line, $800.00 – 900.00.

Pre-1916 Matte Green collection.

3½" vase with handles, $250.00 – 300.00.
4½" round jardiniere, $200.00 – 225.00.
3½" x 6½" vase, $400.00 – 450.00.

8½" six-sided vase, $400.00 – 500.00.
3" x 5" flower bowl, $250.00 – 350.00.

5½" vase, $400.00 – 500.00.
3¼" vase, $250.00 – 350.00.
3½" vase, $350.00 – 450.00.

Great Arts & Crafts piece,
4½" x 11" handled flower bowl, $600.00 – 700.00.

12½" vase, Hunter line,
$1,500.00 – 1,800.00.

5¼" vase, $3,500.00 – 4,000.00.
10" vase, pre-1916, $4,000.00 – 5,000.00.
4" vase, early Matte Ware, $2,000.00 – 3,000.00.

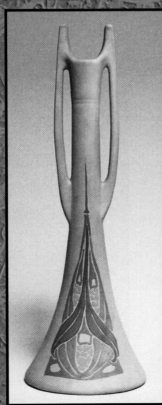

13" vase, $600.00 – 700.00.

14" vase, Arts & Crafts line,
too rare to price.

9½" Tambourine Boy figurine.
This piece of pottery was made by
Sicard in France. He used it as a
sample to get a job with Weller,
$6,000.00 – 9,000.00.

Greora line collection.
4½" vase, $150.00 – 200.00.
9" vase, $400.00 – 500.00.
5" strawberry vase, $175.00 – 225.00.

12" Coppertone jug,
hand thrown, $1,000.00 – 1,200.00.

12" Weller Ware butterfly vase, $350.00 – 450.00.
11½" Silvertone Lily vase, signed "D. E.," $500.00 – 550.00.

7½" octagon-shaped vase, $900.00 – 1,000.00.
11" Eocean vase by Levi Burgess, $800.00 – 900.00.
8½" Rozane vase by Pillsbury, $800.00 – 900.00.

3½" x 12" Ardsley line console bowl, $325.00 – 375.00.
6½" fish flower arranger, $1,000.00 – 1,200.00.

10" x 11" jardiniere, marked "Weller," $800.00 – 1,000.00.

20" Jap Birdimal umbrella stand, $2,100.00 – 2,400.00.
20" Zona line umbrella stand, $2,000.00 – 2,500.00.

16" vase, Dickens Ware, signed by
E. L. Pickens, $3,500.00 – 4,000.00.

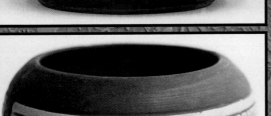

9" California Missions jardiniere,
$700.00 – 800.00.

29½" jardiniere & pedestal,
wonderful fish & bubble design,
$1,700.00 – 2,000.00.

9" fish & bubbles design jardiniere,
$600.00 – 700.00.

17½" Eocean vase,
$900.000 – 1,100.00.

9½" Hudson vase,
$400.00 – 500.00.

20" forest umbrella stand,
$1,900.00 – 2,000.00.

4½" x 7" Woodcraft bowl, $150.00 – 200.00.
9" squirrel wall pocket, $250.00 – 350.00.
5½" x 7" squirrel on bowl, $200.00 – 225.00.

9½" vase, $150.00 – 200.00.
4" x 8" basket, $150.00 – 175.00.
8" forest vase, $250.00 – 300.00.

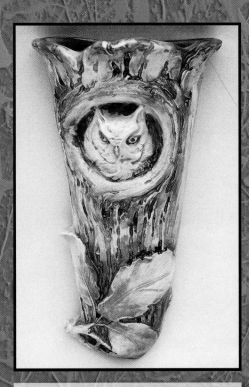

10¼" owl wall pocket, $400.00 – 600.00.

5½" forest pitcher, $125.00 – 175.00.
5¼" vase, $150.00 – 200.00.

8½" nude lady flower arranger, $400.00 – 550.00.
3" x 9" Marvo bowl with flower frog, $300.00 – 400.00.
7" fishing boy flower arranger, $350.00 – 450.00.

9" wall pocket w/plums, $550.00 – 750.00.
12" squirrel wall pocket, $2,200.00 – 2,500.00.
12" apple wall pocket, $750.00 – 950.00.

Woodcraft collection.
9" vase, $150.00 – 200.00.
6" bud vase, $150.00 – 175.00.
9½" vase, $200.00 – 300.00.
8" candlestick, $150.00 – 175.00.
8" double vase, $200.00 – 250.00.

8" jardiniere with birds, $1,500.00 – 1,900.00.
21" Woodcraft floor vase, $2,300.00 – 2,600.00.
7" geese flower frog arranger, $1,200.00 – 1,500.00.

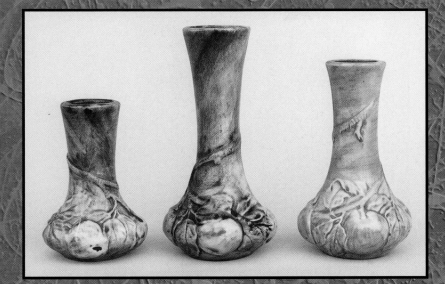

Baldin vase collection.
8" vase, $150.00 – 175.00.
8½" vase, $150.00 – 200.00.
7½" vase, $140.00 – 165.00.

6" Goldenglow vase, $200.00 – 250.00.

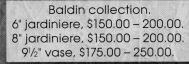

Baldin collection.
6" jardiniere, $150.00 – 200.00.
8" jardiniere, $150.00 – 200.00.
9½" vase, $175.00 – 250.00.

Three nice vases.
10" Woodcraft, $225.00 – 275.00.
7" vase, $150.00 – 200.00.
10" vase, $250.00 – 300.00.

Three wall pockets.
10" Silvertone, $600.00 – 800.00.
8¼" Sabrinian, $500.00 – 600.00.
12" Ardsley, $650.00 – 850.00.

8" Marvo vase, $150.00 – 200.00.
6½" Marvo vase, $100.00 – 150.00.
5" Knifewood vase, $150.00 – 225.00.

6½" vase, $175.00 – 225.00.
8" hanging basket, $125.00 – 175.00.
4" x 6" basket, $150.00 – 225.00.

9½" jardiniere, $175.00 – 225.00.
9" jardiniere, $225.00 – 300.00.

5" x 8" basket, $175.00 – 225.00.
8½" vase, $175.00 – 240.00.
4" x 8" basket, $175.00 – 225.00.

Greenbriar collection.
8" vase, $200.00 – 250.00.
4" vase, $125.00 – 150.00.
7½" vase, $200.00 – 250.00.
5" vase, $135.00 – 165.00.

Blended glaze vases.
6" vase, $150.00 – 200.00.
8" vase, $200.00 – 225.00.

Zona line pitcher collection.
7¾" Strutting Ducks, $200.00 – 250.00.
8" Kingfisher, $300.00 – 400.00.
7" Strutting Ducks, $175.00 – 225.00.

5" Dupont flower bowl,
with removable flower arranger, $150.00 – 200.00.
7½" Creamware jardiniere, $175.00 – 200.00.

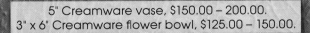

5" Creamware vase, $150.00 – 200.00.
3" x 6" Creamware flower bowl, $125.00 – 150.00.

Wheatley
Cincinnati, Ohio

The Wheatley Pottery Company was established in 1903 by T. J. Wheatley and Isaac Kahn. T. J. Wheatley had previously been associated with other potteries, including his own T. J. Wheatley & Company and, later, Weller pottery. T. J. Wheatley was an accomplished potter who knew all phases of pottery production. The Wheatley Pottery Company made art pottery with green and other matte glazes over relief designs. Wheatley art pottery was produced no later than 1910, when the pottery burned down. It was rebuilt but then began manufacturing architectural ware, tile, and garden pottery. Wheatley died in 1917; the company remained in operation and was purchased in 1927 by the Cambridge Tile Manufacturing Company of Covington, Kentucky.

13½" Matte Green floor vase, $2,400.00 – 2,600.00.
8" x 9" Matte Green floor vase, $1,400.00 – 1,600.00.

Wisecarver
Roseville, Ohio

Rick Wisecarver (1950 – 2003) was an artist and potter from Roseville, Ohio whose work is in the American art pottery tradition. Wisecarver worked with members of his family and with his partner, Richard Sims, to create hand-painted pottery reminiscent of the works of earlier American pottery manufacturers such as Weller and Roseville. Many of his pieces feature the standard glaze of dark browns characteristic of Weller and Roseville pottery produced in the early twentieth century. Wisecarver was a natural artist with no formal training whose first interests were drawing and painting. It was his mother, Bonnie Hoadley, owner of a ceramics shop called Colony House in Roseville, who suggested that Wisecarver paint pottery.

Wisecarver had a great interest in American Indians and created numerous pieces featuring portraits of Indian chiefs, braves, and, less often, Native American women. The pottery is often etched as well as painted.

In addition to Wisecarver's art pottery, he produced a line of cookie jars and many oil paintings on canvases.

He began his pottery career in 1970, at the age of 20, and continued working until his untimely death at the age of 52.

People who purchased pottery from Wisecarver during his lifetime reported that he was sometimes late in completing a promised order. However, he would compensate his customers by delivering an even better or more decorated piece than they had ordered. Interest in Wisecarver's pottery has increased dramatically since his death, and the value of his pottery has risen.

Wisecarver vase collection.
6" vases, $125.00 – 150.00 each.

9" Horseman vase, $300.00 – 350.00,
8" Indian Chief jug, $200.00 – 250.00,
10" Indian Brave jug, $250.00 – 275.00.

Wisecarver pillow vase collection.
9" Indian scene, $375.00 – 475.00.
9" Indian Man & Woman, $350.00 – 450.00.

10" Indian Chief pillow vase, $400.00 – 500.00.
14" Indian Maiden floor vase, $550.00 – 650.00.
11" Indian Man vase, $450.00 – 550.00.

10" Indian Chief vase, $350.00 – 400.00.
11" Indian Brave vase, $625.00 – 700.00,
9" Horseman vase, $350.00 – 400.00.

Photograph of the back sides of
the vases from the photo above.
The Indian Chief & Horseman are the same,
the Indian Brave has a bear painted on the back.

12" pillow vase,
covered bridge scene,
signed by Stephen Wisecarver,
brother to Rick Wisecarver, $350.00 – 500.00.

7" Wisecarver advertising plaque,
$275.00 – 325.00.
10½" Indian Chief vase, $350.00 – 450.00.
9" Indian Chief vase, $350.00 – 425.00.
3" child's mug, $75.00 – 100.00.
Two paperweights, $50.00 each.

9" vase, $400.00 – 500.00.
9" vase, $300.00 – 400.00.
9" vase, $300.00 – 400.00.
8" bottle vase, $400.00 – 500.00.
All hand painted & etched.

9" painted & etched vase, $300.00 – 400.00.
9" Pretty Woman vase, $400.00 – 500.00.
10" painted & etched jardiniere, $300.00 – 400.00.
Bonnie & Clyde painted on the bottom (Rick's parents).

9" etched Indian Chief pillow vase, $350.00 – 450.00.
12½" Indian Brave vase, $400.00 – 500.00.
12½" Indian Brave vase, 400.00 – 500.00.

19" Indian Chief floor vase, $1,000.00 – 1,200.00.
30" jardiniere & pedestal set, hunting bird
dogs scene, $2,000.00 – 3,000.00.

11½" vase with flower scene, $350.00 – 450.00.
12" vase with Indian on horse, etched, $500.00 – 600.00.
10" Indian Chief vase, $400.00 – 500.00.

7" pillow vase with bears, $250.00 – 350.00.
8" pelican figurine, $200.00 – 250.00.
7" pillow vase, African-American, $250.00 – 350.00.

8" pillow vase with Indian chief,
etched, $300.00 – 400.00.
9" pillow vase with Indian chief,
etched, $350.00 – 450.00.
8" bulbous vase with chief,
etched, $400.00 – 500.00.

9" Indian Brave bottle vase, $150.00 – 200.00.
9½" Indian Brave bottle vase, $150.00 – 200.00.
8" Indian Brave bottle vase, $200.00 – 300.00.

14" Cowboy & Saddle, too rare to price.
7½" parrot, $150.00 – 200.00.
10" Cowboy on Bronco, too rare to price.

Three advertising pieces and a Maiden.
For the first two 6" plaques, $200.00 – 250.00.
9" Maiden, $200.00 – 250.00.
5" plaque, $150.00 – 200.00.

Two cookie jars.
12" x 13" Indian Family & Tepee, $400.00 – 450.00.
11½" x 11" Geronimo, $450.00 – 500.00.

13½" crock, $350.00 – 450.00.
10" vase, $400.00 – 500.00.
26½" vase, $1,000.00 – 1,200.00.

21½" floor vase, $1,500.00 – 2,000.00.
21" floor vase, $1,400.00 – 1,800.00.
Last two pieces signed before Wisecarver died.

6½" jug, $250.00 – 300.00.
7" jug, $250.00 – 300.00.
7" jug, $250.00 – 300.00.
5½" vase, $300.00 – 400.00.
5" vase, $250.00 – 300.00.

7½" vase, $300.00 – 400.00.
13" vase, $400.00 – 500.00.
8½" vase, $200.00 – 300.00.

9½" jug, $250.00 – 350.00.
9½" jug, $250.00 – 350.00.
10" jug, $275.00 – 350.00.

8" vase, $200.00 – 300.00.
8" vase, $400.00 – 500.00.
8" bottle vase, $250.00 – 350.00.

11" cookie jar, $250.00 – 300.00.
13" vase, $250.00 – 300.00.

Tankard set.
Two 4½" mugs,
15½" tankard,
7½" sugar & creamer.
$1,200.00 – 1,500.00 set.

9" x 17" Country Doctor
cookie jar, $350.00 – 450.00.

Bibliography

Chipman, Jack. *Collector's Encyclopedia of California Pottery*. Paducah, Kentucky: Collector Books, 1999.

Dommel, Darlene Hurst. *Collector's Encyclopedia of the Dakota Potteries*. Paducah, Kentucky: Collector Books, 1996.

Evans, Paul. *Art Pottery of the United States*. New York: Feingold & Lewis Publishing Corp., 1987.

Gifford, David Edwin. *Collector's Guide to Camark Pottery*. Paducah, Kentucky: Collector Books, 1997.

_____. *Collector's Guide to Camark Pottery, Book II*. Paducah, Kentucky: Collector Books, 1999.

Hanson, Bob, Craig Nissen, and Margaret Hanson. *McCoy Pottery Collector's Reference & Value Guide, Volume I*. Paducah, Kentucky: Collector Books, 1996.

_____. *McCoy Pottery Collector's Reference & Value Guide, Volume II*. Paducah, Kentucky: Collector Books, 1999.

_____. *McCoy Pottery Collector's Reference & Value Guide, Volume III*. Paducah, Kentucky: Collector Books, 2001.

Huxford, Sharon & Bob. *The Collector's Encyclopedia of Brush McCoy Pottery*. Paducah, Kentucky: Collector Books, 1978.

_____. *The Collectors Encyclopedia of Weller Pottery*. Paducah, Kentucky: Collector Books, 1979.

Huxford, Sharon & Bob, and Mike Nickel. *Collector's Encyclopedia of Roseville Pottery, Volume 1*. Paducah, Kentucky: Collector Books, 2001.

_____. *Collector's Encyclopedia of Roseville Pottery, Volume 2*. Paducah, Kentucky: Collector Books, 2001.

James, A. Everette. *North Carolina Art Pottery*. Paducah, Kentucky: Collector Books, 2003.

Karlson, Norman. *American Art Tile*. New York: Rizzoli International Publications, Inc., 1998.

Kovel, Ralph & Terry. *Kovels' American Art Pottery*. New York: Crown Publishers, Inc., 1993.

Lehner, Lois. *Lehner's Encyclopedia of U.S. Marks on Pottery, Porcelain & Clay*. Paducah, Kentucky: Collector Books, 1988.

McDonald, Ann Gilbert. *All About Weller*. Marietta, Ohio: Antique Publications.

Nicholson, Nick & Marilyn, and Jim Thomas. *Rookwood Pottery*. Paducah, Kentucky: Collector Books, 2002.

Peck, Herbert. *The Book of Rookwood Pottery*. New York: Bonanza Books, 1968.

Rago, David. *American Art Pottery*. New York: Knickerbocker Press, 1997.

Rans, Jon and Mark Eckelman. *Collector's Encyclopedia of Muncie Pottery*. Paducah, Kentucky: Collector Books, 1999.

Rans, Jon, Glenn Ralston and Nate Russell. *Zanesville Stoneware Company*. Paducah, Kentucky: Collector Books, 2002.

Reiss, Ray. *Red Wing Art Pottery*. Chicago: Property, 1996.

Roberts, Brenda. *The Collector's Encyclopedia of Hull Pottery*. Paducah, Kentucky: Collector Books, 1980.

Runge, Jr., Robert C. *Collector's Encyclopedia of Stangl Artware, Lamps and Birds, 2nd Edition*. Paducah, Kentucky: Collector Books, 2006.

Sanford, Martha and Steve. *Sanfords' Guide to Peters and Reed*. Adelmore Press, 2000.

Sasicki, Richard, and Josie Fania. *The Collector's Encyclopedia of Van Briggle Art Pottery*. Paducah, Kentucky: Collector Books, 1993.

Sigafoose, Dick. *American Art Pottery*. Paducah, Kentucky: Collector Books, 1998.

Two RumRill Athenian Group bowls and one Rookwood bowl.
5½" x 8½" bowl, $350.00 – 450.00.
7½" x 12" Rookwood bowl, 1927, $650.00 – 750.00.
8½" x 11" bowl, $800.00 – 900.00.

DON'T MISS THESE OTHER GREAT POTTERY TITLES

McCoy POTTERY

Bob Hanson, Craig Nissen & Margaret Hanson

Altogether, these three fabulous books feature over 2,500 full-color photographs of 5,200 pieces made by the Nelson McCoy Pottery Company from 1910 through the 1980s. Over 400 McCoy cookie jars and over 200 wall pockets are showcased. "Finders Keepers" sections highlight pieces that are highly desirable, hard-to-find collectors' items. Volume III boasts a complete index for all three volumes in the series, with all listings including descriptions, eras, sizes, and page numbers on which pieces are featured in each volume. Wall pockets, the Floraline line, cookie jars, gold trim pieces, jardinieres, pedestal sets, lamps, ashtrays, banks, bookend sets, and hundreds more items are featured in these reference guides. Over 150 original catalog pages make these books must-haves for McCoy enthusiasts.

BUY ALL 3 VOLUMES AS A SET & SAVE!!!!!

Volume I · Item #4722 · ISBN: 0-89145-729-1
8½ x 11 · 320 Pgs. · HB · $19.95
Volume II · Item #5268 · ISBN: 1-57432-116-1
8½ x 11 · 304 Pgs. · HB · $24.95
Volume III · Item #5913 · ISBN: 1-57432-252-4
8½ x 11 · 320 Pgs. · HB · $24.95

COLLECTOR BOOKS
P.O. Box 3009 - Paducah, KY 42002-3009

1-800-626-5420

www.collectorbooks.com